Battleground Europe
NORMANDY

GOLD BEACH
INLAND FROM KING

Battleground Europe
NORMANDY

GOLD BEACH
INLAND FROM KING

Christopher Dunphie
and
Garry Johnson

LEO COOPER

COMBINED PUBLISHING
Pennsylvania

Other books by Christopher Dunphie and Garry Johnson
Brightly Shone the Dawn (1980)

Published by
LEO COOPER
an imprint of
Pen Sword Books Limited
47 Church Street, Barnsley, South Yorkshire S70 2AS
Copyright © Christopher Dunphie and Garry Johnson,
1999

ISBN 0 85052 661 2

A CIP catalogue of this book is available
from the British Library

Printed by Redwood Books Limited
Trowbridge, Wiltshire

*For up-to-date information on other titles produced under the Leo Cooper
imprint, please telephone or write to:*
Pen & Sword Books Ltd, FREEPOST, 47 Church Street
Barnsley, South Yorkshire S70 2AS
Telephone 01226 734222

Published under license in the United States of America by

COMBINED PUBLISHING

ISBN 1-58097-008-7

For information, address:
COMBINED PUBLISHING
P.O. Box 307
Conshohocken, PA 19428
E-Mail: combined@dca.net
Web: www.combinedpublishing.com
Orders: 1-800-418-6065

*Cataloging in Publication Data available from the Library of
Congress*

CONTENTS

FOREWORD
by

FIELD MARSHAL THE LORD INGE,
GCB, DL
Chief of the Defence Staff, 1994-1997
Colonel, The Green Howards, 1982-1994

This is an excellent little book with some powerful messages. It is certainly more than merely a very good battlefield guide. I hope that it will be read by a much wider audience than just those with an interest in military history in general and the Normandy Invasion of June 1944 in particular.

I was fortunate enough to attend several Staff College Battlefield Tours which formed such an important part in the Staff College's programme. I learnt something of importance every year. The tours, as the authors have made clear, were not designed to deal with military strategy or tactics, but rather to bring out some of the realities of war at the sharp end. The success of the tours was due to the wonderful team of 'guest artists', many of whose stories are told here. This book will be a small but permanent recognition of the debt which I and many thousands of Army Staff College students owe to this special group of men, who told their stories with great modesty and humility, but with an epic quality.

There are many lessons to be learnt from the stories told, but there are two which to me stand out above all others. First, as the authors have said, 'the actions of one man who imposes himself on the situation can spell the difference between success and failure'. Second is the critical importance of firm, robust leadership, without which no campaign can ever be won. I only hope that in this era of instant media analysis, political correctness and litigation which seems to follow in its wake, we are not in danger of breeding bureaucratic managers rather than commanders prepared to take risks.

On a personal basis, this book gives me enormous pleasure

on two accounts. The first is because my Regiment played such a key part in the Normandy campaign with Company Sergeant Major Stanley Hollis winning the only VC awarded on D-Day. Secondly because in Chapter 7, dealing with Villers-Bocage, it tells the story of the 1st/7th Queens, commanded by Lieutenant-Colonel Desmond Gordon, a Green Howard who later became a Major-General and Colonel of my Regiment. As a very junior officer I was fortunate enough to be his ADC. There is no-one to whom I owe a greater debt. He was a wonderful mentor to me from the time I was an Officer Cadet at RMA Sandhurst until I retired.

The authors praise, in Chapter 3, the Green Howards' newly erected War Memorial at Crépon. I believe that the sculptor, James Butler, has managed quite brilliantly to sculpt a soldier who, at the end of D-Day, is reflecting: 'It has been quite a day. I have lost many of my friends and a lot of action lies ahead of me'. This memorial would not have been possible without the initiative of Mr Ian Homersham and the great personal generosity of Sir Ernest Harrison, who in addition bought CSM Hollis' VC and gave it to the Regiment. As Sir Ernest said, 'That is where I and my family believe it belongs'.

Finally, I would like to congratulate Christopher Dunphie and Garry Johnson on producing this splendid book. I commend it to all young Army officers – and Ministers of Defence!

Peter Inge

June 1999

Richmond,
North Yorkshire.

7

INTRODUCTION

Every year, from 1947 to 1979, the Directing Staff and students of the Army Staff College at Camberley travelled to Normandy in June. There they sprawled in groups in the long grass and listened to the stories of some of those who fought in the 1944 Normandy campaign.

This was neither a holiday nor an exercise in nostalgia, though it was certainly a welcome break in a year of intensive study. It was, in fact, an essential part in the education of young Army officers, who might in future years hold senior command and staff appointments. Strategy and tactics could be learned from books or military training, but it is difficult to impart a true understanding of the reality of battle. Many post-war soldiers have faced low-level action – the terrorist, armed with rifle or bomb. But, with the exception of Korea in the early 1950s, none have fought in an extended full-scale war. The Falklands and Gulf conflicts, demanding as they were, hardly produced opposition like the German Panzer Divisions in Normandy in 1944. What is it like when your tank squadron's advance is suddenly confronted by 88mm guns, which can knock you out long before your own weapons come into range? How do men react to prolonged shelling? What are the effects on the human spirit of the stress of combat? How do you overcome your own quite natural fear and lead men in action – not just once, but day after day? What happens when the chaos of the battlefield disrupts the neat plans of commanders and their staffs? All these, and many others, were questions to which the students found answers, often hidden in the stories which unfolded on those annual Battlefield Tours.

One important lesson, which emerged so clearly but which can never be reproduced on training away from the danger of live ammunition, is that there are moments when the pendulum of battle seems to hang limp; when a strong personality, be he Colonel, Corporal or even Private Soldier, grabs that pendulum and pulls it firmly his way. The significance of the actions of one man, who imposes his personality on the situation at a critical moment, can spell the difference between success and failure. Equally certainly, the commander who, for any of a number of reasons, cannot provide the clear and dynamic leadership

Over one hundred concrete caissons were towed across the Channel and positioned off the French coast at Omaha and Gold beaches forming artificial harbours.

which the situation and his men demand, will fail. The significance of the individual was a lesson which emerged at almost every 'stand'.

The men who, on those annual visits, described their personal experiences of battle, on the very ground where the actions had taken place, had found their own answers the hard way. It would have been easy to have labelled them as 'heroes'; a label which all would have strongly resented. They saw themselves as ordinary men in an extraordinary situation. They told their stories with humility and humour. The student returned from a tour not just fascinated by the stories he had heard, but quietly reassured that perhaps, if the call came to him

Piers in operation with floating roadways (to the left) leading to the shore at Arromanches.

and his generation, he might answer that call as had those who went to Normandy in 1944.

In 1980, to mark the end of the annual Staff College Battlefield Tours, we produced a small book, *Brightly Shone the Dawn*, which aimed to record a few of those stories, lest they fade away, with the passage of time, into unrecorded history. Some of those stories are reproduced here, for the most part updated by more research.

This book does not seek to be a comprehensive history of the Normandy Campaign, nor even of the events *Inland from King Beach*. Rather it is a collection of inter-linked snapshots of specific incidents on the route inland. The dedicated student of military history will find many books which give a far fuller account of the campaign. Our aim is to take the visitor who wants to understand something of the individual in war, and lead him to specific places on the ground where he may capture something of just a few of the personalities and events of the 1944 battlefields.

For those who decide to follow this story on the ground we suggest that the best place from which to start your pilgrimage is the delightful seaside town of Arromanches. Nestling in a small cove among the hills, it may seem an unlikely startpoint – until one notices the remains of the Mulberry Harbour off-shore. Throughout the summer of 1944 Arromanches was the vital lifeline through which reinforcements, stores and all the

A Sherman tank begins its journey to the fighting, travelling along one of the floating roadways connecting the piers with the shore at Arromanches.

necessary paraphernalia of war had to come, and through which casualties and prisoners of war returned to Britain, as the Armies inland fought to expand their D Day beach-head and in due course break-out to liberate France and defeat Germany.

During the planning for D Day it was assumed that any port that might be captured would be mined and its handling facilities destroyed. The very concept of constructing mobile ports and floating them across the Channel is almost unthinkable today, even with more than half a century of advances in technology. And yet more than two million tons of prefabricated steel and concrete were concealed off the coast of Southern England, towed across to Normandy and constructed into the two Mulberry Harbours at Arromanches and St Laurent (Omaha Beach – destroyed in a storm 19-22 June). The outer breakwaters consisted of aged ships which were steamed into position before being sunk. In addition vast concrete caissons were towed across the Channel and sunk. Many can still be seen off the coast at Arromanches today, particularly at low tide. Inside these protected areas floating piers were positioned, so that ships could moor and unload. From these piers sections of floating roadways, which had been towed into position and bolted together, linked piers to beaches. By the end of August 1944, when the Battle of Normandy had been won, the 2nd British Army numbered some 830,000 men, with 203,000 vehicles and 1,240,000 tonnes of stores, much of which had come through Arromanches. The magnitude of this achievement

can best be understood by a visit to the excellent museum at Arromanches, with its working models, films, etc. Arromanches is indeed an admirable launch-pad from which to follow the incidents covered by this book.

Some will read this small book in the comfort of their homes, perhaps in front of a blazing fire on a cold winter's evening, with a glass in their hand and a map of Normandy beside them. We hope that they will glean something of those whose stories we have tried to tell. But the real value of this book should be for those who can give a day or two to visit the battlefields, to stand where they stood in the fields and lanes of Normandy, and to hear the voices of those young men who, answering the call of Duty, found themselves plunged into an extraordinary adventure which would alter their lives and outlooks and chart the course of history. They are elderly now, those who are left, and we should remember them and their comrades with pride, grateful for the peace they won for us.

We would particularily like to record our thanks to those who have allowed us to retell their stories. Many of those listed below are, sadly, no longer alive, but, whether in 1980 or 1999, we greatly appreciate the help they gave us:

Major-General Sir James d'Avigdor-Goldsmid, Bt, CB, OBE, MC.
Captain PGC Dickens, DSO, MBE, DSC.
Captain P Dyas, OBE.
Major-General DS Gordon, CB, CBE, DSO, DL.
Lieutenant Colonel RHWS Hastings, DSO, OBE, MC.
Company Sergeant Major SE Hollis, VC.
Lieutenant Commander HM Irwin, VRD, RNVR.
Major CF Milner, MC.
General Sir John Mogg, GCB, CBE, DSO, DL.
Captain AMcL Morrison, MC.

We are grateful Gavin Waddell who drew the maps, and to Michael Irwin who has allowed us to use some of the photographs he took on D-Day.

Finally, we would ask anyone who does visit these battlefields to give time to visit at least one of the many War Cemeteries in Normandy. No true Battlefield Tour could be complete without paying one's respect to those who answered the call, but did not return.

June 1999

Bridge of Cally,　　　　　　Winchester,
Perthshire.　　　　　　　　Hampshire.

CHAPTER ONE

OPERATION OVERLORD

During the early summer of 1944 the Western Allies gathered their strength for the great enterprise which was to liberate occupied Europe and end in the conquest of Nazi Germany. In the armed camps of southern England, where the invasion forces gathered, men's eyes and thoughts turned southward to France. Three great questions were in all minds: where would it happen, and when, and, above all, what would it be like over there?

Across the Channel the German propaganda magazine *Signal* featured pictures of strong, confident troops gazing resolutely seaward from their emplacements on the Atlantic Wall. Hitler boasted with his usual confidence that Fortress Europe was impregnable.

On the face of it the German strength was formidable. Field Marshal von Rundstedt, as Commander-in-Chief West, was responsible for the defence of France, Belgium and Holland, and had more than half a million men under his command for the task. These troops were organised into two Army Groups, with 38 infantry divisions guarding the coastline and a further 10 held in reserve. A Panzer Group of 10 armoured and mechanised division were also stationed in France. The defences along the Channel coast were a monument to German efficiency and hard work. The beaches were cluttered with ingenious death-traps. Obstacles of varying shape and size, many carrying explosive charges and designed to impede the movement of landing craft, vehicles and men, covered the shores like barnacles, from Antwerp to the Cherbourg peninsula. These obstacles were covered at approximately 1,000-metre intervals by mutually supporting strongpoints formed from concrete emplacements, surrounded by barbed wire and mines. Each contained artillery pieces, anti-tank and machine guns and a garrison of between 50 and 200 men. The strongpoints were linked by anti-tank ditches. All roads leading off the beaches were blocked and the low-lying areas were flooded. Interspersed with the strongpoints were 20 huge

Atlantic Wall defenders – an NCO puts his men through their paces.

coastal batteries between Cherbourg and Le Havre. Each battery, with its huge concrete casemates, was a fortress in its own right. The Saint Marcouf Battery, for example, contained three 210 mm guns with a range of 27 km, six anti-aircraft guns, one 150 mm and four 20 mm guns, two mortars, numerous flame-throwers and machine guns and a garrison of three officers, seven non-commissioned officers and 287 men. In support further inland were medium and field artillery regiments, and the reserve divisions. The villages behind the beaches were fortified with blockhouses, the roads were mined and the fields covered with long poles to prevent gliders from landing.

Impressive though the static positions were, there were flaws in the German defence. The troops themselves were not of top quality. By this stage of the war Russia and Italy were draining German manpower and the divisions in the West contained large numbers of semi-invalids, recruits and pressed foreigners.

The Luftwaffe, too, was low in strength and quality. The Third Air Fleet, based in France, numbered only 160 aircraft. Finally, the German High Command was riven with controversy over how the impending battle should be fought. Field Marshal Rommel, in command of Army Group B in the northern part of von Rundstedt's command, firmly believed that the Allies should be defeated on the beaches before their vanguard could gain a stronghold on the Continent. A strange turn of tactics for the man who had been a master of mobile warfare in the desert, but Rommel had felt the devastating effect of air superiority at the receiving end and knew that mobile reserves would be severely hampered on a battlefield over which the Allied aircraft flew virtually unmolested. So Rommel asked for the Panzer divisions to be allocated to the Atlantic Wall. Von Rundstedt disagreed. Influenced by his experience in outflanking the Maginot line with the help of Luftwaffe supremacy in 1940 and not fully accepting the complete reversal of circumstances which now applied, von Rundstedt pressed for the classic military solution of not committing the reserves until the direction of the enemy thrust was confirmed. The result, at Hitler's direction, was a compromise. On D-Day Rommel had one Panzer division in his reserve (the 21st), while three more were held under orders, not even of von Rundstedt, but of Hitler himself.

An important factor in the German arguments over how best to group their forces was the question of where the Allies would land. Security was strict and the only information reaching the Germans was that which the Allies wanted them to have. There were two possible areas for the invasion force to land. The Pas de Calais, opposite the Kentish coast, offered the obvious advantages of a short sea crossing and a short flying time from home airfields for covering fighter aircraft. Normandy was further away but had various factors in its favour. One of the most important of them was that if the Allies were to succeed it would be vital for them to have the use of port facilities for supply and troop build-up early in the battle. The unsuccessful raid on Dieppe in 1942 had shown how heavily defended were all the French ports. A solution was found in the creation of Mulberry Harbours which would be towed across the Channel and sunk off the French coast to form harbours as large as that of Dover. The beaches at the Pas de Calais were unsuitable for such a scheme, but the long, shelving sands of Normandy, protected from the worst of the Atlantic weather by the Cherbourg peninsula, were ideal. The decision was for Normandy. The need now was to persuade the Germans that the Pas de Calais had been selected.

The art of deception is, of course, that of persuading your opponent that you will undertake Course A, when in fact you plan to follow Course B. The best chance of achieving this is to find out what he wants to believe, convince him he is correct, and then do actually something quite different. This is the story of the D-Day Deception Plan – Operation Fortitude.

Fortitude North involved 'creating', largely through simulated radio traffic, a fictitious Army in Scotland, which might in theory pose a threat to Norway. The success of Fortitude North is shown by the fact that it was not until 16 June that the Germans removed any troops from Norway – too late to affect the battle in northern France.

From Ultra intercept it was clear that the Germans expected the invasion to come at the Pas de Calais. Fortitude South was designed to confirm this impression in German minds. To achieve this a fictitious 1st US Army Group (FUSAG) was 'invented', commanded by the flamboyant US General George Patton, who was frequently photographed 'inspecting troops in south-east England'. Tanks, vehicles, camps and store parks, not quite well enough camouflaged to avoid detection, were in fact inflatable dummies, as were the landing-craft which mushroomed along the banks of the Thames and Medway. And the radio traffic necessary to support the daily life of FUSAG, as it trained and prepared to invade the Pas de Calais area of northern France, was easily heard by the Germans eagerly listening across the Channel, confirming them in their views.

By late 1942 the British had arrested every spy that the Germans had tried to infiltrate into Britain. Many had been 'turned' and were now working for the Allies, feeding false information, about formations such as FUSAG, to their former masters.

Nor could the Deception Plan end with D-Day itself. The longer the Germans could be persuaded, after D-Day, that there was still a real threat elsewhere than Normandy, the slower they might be to move forces to confront the Normandy invasion. So successful was this plan that on 10 July, five weeks after D-Day and only two weeks before the break-out from the beach-head, a signal from Rommel to von Rundstedt stated:

> *'The enemy has at present 35 divisions in the landing area. In Great Britain another 60 divisions are standing-by, 50 of which may at any moment be transferred to the continent. We shall have to reckon with large scale landings of 1 US Army Group in the north for strategic co-operation with the Montgomery Army Group in a thrust on Paris.'*

Some of these divisions did exist, but were destined for Normandy. Others did not. FUSAG, and the threat it posed to the Pas de Calais never actually existed.

The date and time of the landing was, to a large extent, determined by Rommel himself. The Army planners wished to land in darkness or at dawn when the greatest tactical surprise could be achieved, but the Navy pressed for a daylight assault, allowing for greater control of shipping and of the naval and air bombardment. In the event, beach reconnaissance showed that Rommel's obstacles were submerged at high water and that it would be necessary to carry out demolition work on them at low tide and in daylight. It was finally agreed that the landings would take place, after a moonlit night, about 10 minutes after

The Allied Command Team. From the left: General Bradley (First US Army); Admiral Ramsay (C-in-C Naval Forces); Air Chief Marshal Tedder (Deputy Supreme Commander); General Eisenhower (Supreme Commander); General Montgomery (C-in-C Land Forces); Air Chief Marshal Leigh-Mallory (C-in-C Air Forces); General Bedell Smith (Eisenhower's Chief of Staff).

sunrise and two to three hours after low tide. Such a precise requirement could only be met on about three days in every lunar month. This, combined with other factors, dictated that D-Day should take place in the first week of June 1944.

The idea of the invasion had been in Churchill's mind since the dark days of 1940 when survival, rather than conquest, had been the uppermost consideration in most Englishmen's minds. 'Nous reviendrons', he had told the French, 'We shall be back'. A Planning team, COSSAC (Chief of Staff to the Supreme Allied Commander-designate), was established in May 1943 under the British Lieutenant General Morgan, tasked with conducting research and planning for D-Day. Three months later COSSAC submitted its initial plan – an invasion by three divisions between Ouistreham and Grandchamp, on the Normandy coast, supported by an airborne division on Caen.

In December 1943 General Eisenhower was appointed Supreme Commander, with Air Chief Marshal Tedder as his deputy and General Montgomery commanding the landing forces, 21st Army Group. Montgomery considered the invasion area to be too narrow and the force too small. In consequence the plan was expanded to a five division assault, with three airborne divisions deployed on the flanks. General Bradley's 1st US Army would land at Utah and Omaha Beaches in the west, with 4 Infantry Division at Utah at the foot of the Cotentin Peninsula, and 1 Infantry Division, backed by 29 Infantry Division at Omaha. Utah would be the launch-pad for subsequent operations to cut the Cotentin Peninsula, isolate and then capture Cherbourg, thereby hopefully providing a workable port. To ensure success, 82 and 101 Airborne Divisions would be dropped inland from Utah, in the area of Sainte Mère-Eglise, to protect the flanks of the Utah force and secure crossings over the flooded Merderet valley which would be needed during a speedy break-out from the beach area. General Dempsey's 2nd British Army would land at Gold, Juno and Sword Beaches in the east, with 50 Infantry Division at Gold, 3 Canadian Infantry Division at Juno and 3 Infantry Division at Sword. At the extreme eastern end 6 Airborne Division would secure a small bridgehead east of the River Orne, between Caen and the sea. The landing area would spread along fifty miles of the Normandy coast, with a boundary between the two armies in the area of Port-en-Bessin.

Amphibian Wing of the Royal Army Service Corps preparing for the invasion, seen here in sand dunes somewhere in England. Just a small part of the vast Allied force training to use new-fangled specialists vehicles – in this case, the DUKW.

Throughout May 1944 the south of England became one huge military cantonment containing 39 divisions (20 American, 14 British, 3 Canadian, 1 French and 1 Polish). These were supported by 5,049 fighter aircraft, 3,467 heavy bombers, 2,343 other combat aircraft, 2,316 transport aircraft and 2,591 gliders. More than 6,000 warships, merchant vessels and landing craft were assembled to transport the force. There were also specialist tanks carrying flails for minefield clearance, mats for covering sandy beaches, bridges for crossing gaps, amphibious tanks with propellers, 70 old merchant ships and 4 warships to sink as breakwaters, 2 artificial harbours, and a cross-channel pipe-line for supplying petrol (PLUTO) until the tankers could berth. 66,000 tons of bombs were dropped on Normandy during the three months preceding D-Day, creating what Churchill called 'a railway desert' around the Germans. This preparatory work was to be strengthened by a further 14,000 tons dropped on radar installations on the eve of D-Day and by a massive air and sea bombardment prior to and during the landings.

As the great day drew near General Montgomery visited his troops in southern England, briefing large gatherings on the forthcoming operation. With soldierly brevity he summed it all up in a few simple words:

'We have a long sea journey, and at the end of it all we will have to land on an enemy coast in the face of determined opposition. The violence, speed and power of our initial assault must carry everything before it.'

The dawn was about to break.

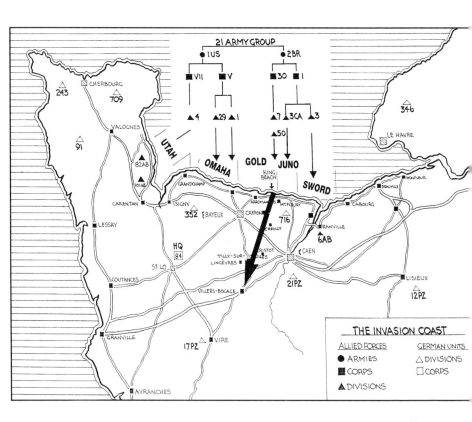

CHAPTER TWO

THE NAVAL SPRINGBOARD

A certain knowledge that he and his ship were to take part in the making of history was what most impressed Lieutenant Peter Dickens, as he sailed HMS *Blencathra*, a Hunt class destroyer, from her normal patrol station on the east coast of England towards Milford Haven. He had not been told why he must report there, but clearly something big was in the wind. This was one of the most extraordinary facts about Operation Overlord – everybody, both allies and enemy, knew that it was imminent, yet the details remained one of the best kept secrets of the war.

As she ploughed through the English Channel, *Blencathra* passed a tug towing what Dickens later described as 'a vast and half-submerged cotton reel'. Unable to control his inquisitiveness, Dickens signalled the tug's captain, asking what it was. 'A machine for putting a head on watery wartime beer!' came the splendidly misleading reply, with which Dickens had to be content as he made his way onwards towards his destination. Only later, after the invasion, did he learn about PLUTO – Pipe Line Under The Ocean.

Two parcels awaited him at Milford Haven. The smaller contained the detailed orders for Operation Neptune, the naval assault. Dickens handled these reverently. The larger contained the amendments, and since security ordained that only the Captain should see them he settled down for a lengthy session

HMS Blencathra, a Hunt class destroyer commanded by Peter Dickens on D-Day.

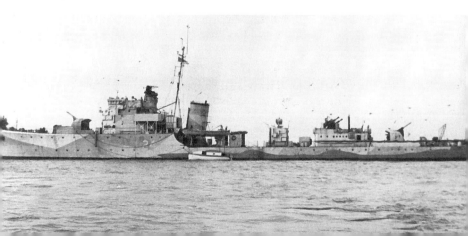

'The sea was filled with shipping of all shapes and sizes' – headiong for the coast of France.

with scissors, paste and waste-paper basket. As he worked through the orders, he began to understand the true magnitude of the operation. The complete confidence in victory; the amazing detail; all truly staggered him. The little *Blencathra* would be just one ship among almost 7,000, yet, as he read on, it was made perfectly clear what he was required to do and how his small part would fit into the whole complex jigsaw.

The waste-paper basket soon filled, and when Dickens was momentarily in the 'heads' his ever solicitous steward, Able Seaman Gallop, ditched the entire contents into the fast-ebbing tide. Not just a few slips of paper, but whole pages, even chapters, all marked 'TOP SECRET', top and bottom, front and back. Horror dawned quickly. 'Action Stations. Away Life-boats crews'. And soon these were seen busily harvesting their catch of soggy paper. Quite what the natives of Milford Haven thought of this sudden maritime 'Keep Britain Tidy' campaign is not recorded, but at least the Germans never found out. Nor, which was perhaps just as important, did Dickens' admiral!

Blencathra was not one of the first echelon of assaulting ships. She sailed on D-Day as part of the escort to an American follow-up convoy, and arrived off Utah beach on D+1. Dickens described the passage as 'uneventful', meaning only that there was no enemy action. But then he was convinced that there would be none; the orders had more or less said so. But if

uneventful from the point of view of action, it was indeed eventful, even inspiring, by other standards. As *Blencathra* neared the Spout, the point where the coastal channels merged and headed south through the cleared minefield lanes, the sea was filled with shipping of all shapes and sizes and in such numbers that chaos seemed inevitable. Yet each group could be identified in the book, and all seemed to be at the right place and time. The minefield channels were clearly marked by buoys, and it was the job of the escorts to keep the transports between them, even though this apparently simple manoeuvre was easier said than done, since some of the less professional sailors, unused to the strong cross tides, did not readily appreciate the need both to steer crabwise and to keep station on a line of bearing.

From the moment that the leading landing-craft lowered its doors and the assaulting infantry and tanks struggled through the surf onto the beaches, the focus of attention inevitably switched from sea to land. But the Navy's task was by no means over – indeed it had only just begun. The soldiers fighting inland would need thousands of tons of stores, ammunition and equipment. There would be a constant flow of casualties and prisoners moving back to England, and replacements moving out. And as the Allied armies strengthened and expanded their hold on French soil, so more formations would be fed in, before the beach-head, bulging like an overfull balloon, would burst, and the advance which would lead to the final defeat of Hitler's

A landing craft fills with GIs destined for Utah beach on D+1. HMS *Blencathra* was one of the escort vessels.

Landing craft pass one of the bombarding warships.

Germany, would begin. Everything must be brought across the Channel from England, and be landed in the early stages over the open beaches and later through the Mulberry Harbour at Arromanches. The security of this, the Army's lifeline, was the Navy's task in the weeks following D-Day.

HMS *Blencathra* delivered her charges safely to Utah Beach on D+1 and, following instructions, steamed east towards the British assault area. The sight, along the 25 mile journey, was remarkable. The concentration of ships of all shapes and sizes stretched from horizon to horizon; battleships, cruisers, destroyers, all firing desultorily from one end while sailors not on duty sunbathed at the other; transports, freighters, tankers, minesweepers, a wide variety of specialised ships; landing ships and of course hundreds of landing craft which buzzed between ship and beach like bees between heather and hive. Each ship carried some vital equipment or fulfilled some crucial function which would help the armies now ashore. The shells that sped inland did so in response to some urgent request for fire support. Unseen in the bowels of the bombarding ships men pored over maps, calculated range, elevation and direction, transmitted orders and corrections to those manning the gun turrets – all in support of the soldiers fighting inland.

Dickens weaved his way through this maze to make the appointed rendezvous with his admiral. Finding him at the correct place, of course, he was told of his role in the protection of this vast armada. This seemed an almost irrelevant task – was it possible that a force of this size could be vulnerable to any form of German attack? As he watched the continual stream of aircraft overhead, Dickens reflected that it was four years almost to the day that the Luftwaffe had owned the skies over Dunkirk. Now they could muster little over 100 fighters to oppose the 5,000 which the Allies could put into the air over the invasion area.

But war is always a story of the unexpected. And so it was that on one fine evening as *Blencathra* was going out on patrol, Dickens was standing on the bridge idly watching an aircraft weaving its way through the forest of masts when it made a sudden dart towards him, and he woke up just in time to order 'Full ahead; hard a-starboard', as the track of a torpedo slid a few feet past his hull.

'I sweated, not so much with terror as with abject shame.

After five solid years of fighting! I resolved never to take anything for granted again. The plane flew off with smoke pouring from its engines; the mixture must have needed adjusting or something – nothing to do with our gunnery!'

Each night the eastern end of the anchorage was guarded by a line of Landing Craft (Gun), and the northern edge by minesweepers, all at anchor. Ouside these, motor gunboats patrolled, controlled by radar-fitted frigates. Further out, the Hunt class destroyers, operating in pairs, supported them. A few German motor torpedo boats made several gallant sorties against ridiculous odds. But, for the most part, the nights were dull, because 'there were never enough enemy torpedo boats to go round'. And after a particularily effective air raid on their base at Le Havre on 14 June, they virtually ceased to function.

One night, however, when two sizeable ships were detected leaving the Seine and heading north at high speed, Dickens resolved to investigate:

'I set out with my sister ship, Quorn, whose First Lieutenant just happened to be my brother. We hadn't gone far when our deviation became apparent to the flagship which pompously told me to 'resume your appointed station'. But Nelson's blind-eye technique seemed appropriate and we pressed on. Alas, the enemy was faster than us and we couldn't make it; but what we did make was the range of the German heavy battery at Cap d'Antifer, and when we were surrounded by splashes rather higher than the mast my mind became wonderfully concentrated and duty suddenly became a pleasure!'

One unorthodox weapon which the Germans tried against the Allied fleet was the 'human torpedo'. This was, in fact, two torpedoes; a real one, with a warhead, slung below another which was little more than an engine with a cockpit in which the luckless driver was confined for perhaps 12 hours – or the rest of his life, whichever was shortest. It could do only 2 or 3 knots, and was undetectable by Asdic (anti submarine detection device). One night the Germans released a mass of these from the east of the assault area, when the tide was west-running. The first that Dickens heard was a signal from a neighbouring patrol saying *Quorn* sunk, no survivors'.

'That was a blow; you know how it is with brothers. You don't really miss them till they're not around. As soon as I could leave my patrol at dawn I went over there as a sort of last rite, but on

the way a human torpedo suddenly appeared alongside, with the driver still on board. I thought that if we picked him up he would sink the wretched thing as he got out, and that we ought to try to take it back for the Intelligence people to play around with. So we hoisted it on board, with him still inside. When we released him from his cockpit he told us that he had set the demolition charges, which would go off in a matter of seconds. Luckily someone understood German and we all dived behind the funnel. After a huge explosion there wasn't a piece of that torpedo left larger than a saucepan, but we found out that dozens of the things had been washed up on the beaches anyway."

Lieutenant Peter Dickens, RN, in 1944.

Quorn was there alright, a double echo on the Asdic. Nothing else. So Dickens turned disconsolately back towards his anchorage. On his arrival, and to his intense relief, his brother turned up in a small craft. *Quorn* had split in two and sunk quickly, but he had floated off the bridge. The lifebuoy sentry on the near vertical stern had managed to set all the depth charges to safe, so that they would not go off as the ship went down, and had then stepped dry-shod onto the only boat that was there. *Quorn's* consort had stopped initially, but, when narrowly missed by a torpedo herself, had wisely moved off. There were only 35 survivors out of a ship's complement of 170 – one of those all too frequent wasteful incidents in war which does not affect the outcome of the battle. Dickens' brother had spent many hours in the water, holding on to men who were holding on to men who were holding on to a Carley raft. Some prayed; others called for

'Mum'; one just floated away and drowned, not because he was weak but because he was just plain angry.

But for Dickens and the rest of the Navy life remained busy, if unexciting. The action had moved into the Normandy countryside as the soldiers fought their way inland.

Inland from King Beach. A map to support the directions given in the text.

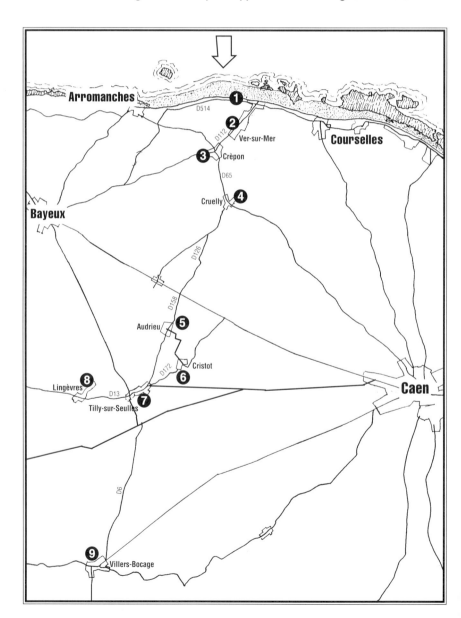

CHAPTER THREE

KING BEACH - 0725 D DAY

Gold Beach, the D Day assault objective of 50th (Northumbrian) Division, was subdivided into two – Jig and King. Major General Douglas Graham, 50 Division's commander, had four brigades under command. On the right 231 Brigade, with 56 Brigade behind, would assault Jig Beach; on the left 69 Brigade, backed by 151 Brigade, would land at King Beach. These two beaches were each subdivided into Green (right) and Red (left). Within 69 Brigade, 6th Battalion The Green Howards would land on King Green, 5th Battalion East Yorkshire Regiment on King Red.

It is worth noting the outline timings immediately before and after H Hour, which give some impression of the thoroughness of the planning and the weight of resources involved. These were much the same for all the British beaches.

H-7 hours: RAF bombers start attacks on the German positions, and in particular on the ten main coastal batteries.

H-75 minutes: RAF bombing ceases – after 1,316 sorties, dropping 5,853 tons of bombs.

H-60 minutes: US Air Force bomb beach defences – 1,083 sorties, 7,348 tons. Naval Bombardment Groups (6 battleships, 2 monitors, 22 cruisers) fire on the larger coastal batteries. Smaller ships engage beach defences.

H-15 minutes: Landing Craft (Rocket) open fire – 20,000 rockets fall on British beaches. Self-propelled artillery (25-pounder Sexton armoured vehicles) open fire from landing craft as they come within range of the shore.

H-5 minute DD tanks (amphibious Shermans with canvas flotation screens and Duplex Drive propellors) swim ashore.

H Hour: Assault engineers mine and obstacle clearance vehicles touch down.

H+7 minutes: Assault battalions go ashore, in two waves.

H+45 minutes: Reserve battalions land, followed by successive waves bearing naval beach control parties, infantry Bren-gun carriers and self-propelled anti-tank guns (US M10 armoured vehicles with 17-pounder guns), Crocodile tanks (flame-throwers), reserve tanks (non-amphibious Shermans) and beach trackway equipment.

H+90 minutes: Self-propelled artillery lands, followed by towed artillery and anti-tank guns.

For the most part the sheer weight of fire and strength of the assault force overwhelmed the German beach defences. Only on Omaha beach, where the Americans found far stronger defences than anticipated and where the assaulting divisions were pinned on the beaches until the afternoon, did the Germans manage seriously to disrupt the landings. And with Allied mastery of the sky, the German Air Force hardly put in an appearance. Montgomery's call for 'the violence, speed and power of the initial assault' was well heeded.

Lieutenant Colonel Robin Hastings walked down Whitehall on a fine morning in March 1944. The trees were already in bud;

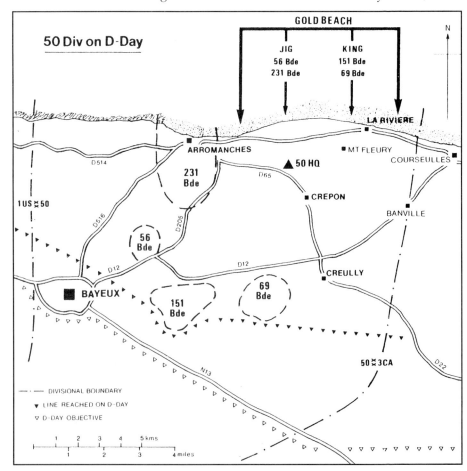

the promise of Spring evident. Great events, in war as well as in nature, were clearly imminent, and Hastings was on his way to the War Office to be told the part that his battalion, 6th Battalion The Green Howards, would play in the forthcoming invasion.

The Green Howards was, and still is, a Yorkshire regiment. Although a Territorial rather than a Regular Army battalion, the 6th Battalion was already battle-experienced. It had taken part in the 1940 campaign which ended ignominiously at Dunkirk, had fought in the 8th Army's desert campaign and been one of the assault battalions for the invasion of Sicily. To replace some of those lost in France and the Mediterranean, the battalion had received large numbers of reinforcements, many of whom came from outside Yorkshire. Indeed Hastings himself was one of those 'imported' from another regiment. He had served with distinction in The Rifle Brigade throughout the Desert campaign, winning a Military Cross and two Mentions in Despatches, and had already been 'noticed' by many senior Generals, including Montgomery, as a young leader of real distinction. He was just 26 years old when he assumed command of 6 Green Howards in Sicily in July 1943. But although so many of those who, like Hastings, now wore The Green Howards cap-badge in 1944 came from other regiments and other parts of Britain, 6 Green Howards never lost its Yorkshire ethos.

After some hours in the bowels of the War Office, Hastings emerged. His mind raced as, on his journey to rejoin his men in Scotland, he ran over the details of the task ahead of them. To be one of the leading battalions ashore on D Day seemed a sufficient challenge. But, having captured his allotted stretch of beach and destroyed its defences, including some potentially troublesome pill-boxes, the Yorkshiremen had to move inland and capture a prominent house with a circular drive. Next, just behind this house, the battalion must put out of action the Mont Fleury gun battery – vast concrete emplacements at present being hastily thrown up to house 150mm guns which could wreak fearful damage upon the ships stationed off the beaches and the soldiers who would wade ashore. A further mile inland, the Meuvaines Ridge and a suspected rocket site were to be captured, with the help of the tanks of 4th/7th Royal Dragoon Guards. Even this was not the end. They must then advance almost ten miles inland and capture an important ridge near St Léger, astride the Caen-Bayeux road. The country through which they would advance was a mass of small fields and orchards, high hedges, narrow sunken lanes and tiny hamlets. This was the 'bocage'. With trees and hedges clad in the heavy foliage of June it would be a defender's paradise. The horizon would seldom be further than 100 yards, and a few resolute men with a Spandau machine-gun could hold up an advance of a sizeable force for hours, causing heavy casualties. The nine mile walk from King Beach to St Léger seemed a very long way, mused Hastings as he journeyed north, even without the added 'bonus' of every hedge concealing someone intent on stopping you.

To carry out this demanding list of tasks, Hastings had his own battalion of four rifle companies, with a support company of mortars and machine guns. He was also allocated the Sherman tanks of B Squadron 4th/7th Royal Dragoon Guards, two teams of Royal Engineers AVREs (Armoured Vehicle Royal Engineers) and Flails. [The AVRE, was a converted Churchill tank with a 290mm Petard mortar, which fired a bunker-busting high-explosive 'dustbin' over a distance of about 80 yards. It could also carry rolls of track matting (Bobbins) or bundles of chestnut paling (Fascines) for filling craters in roads. The Flail was a Sherman tank which had a drum fixed between two extended arms. As the drum rotated numerous chains would 'flail' the way through a minefield clearing a path about 9 foot wide.] Also there was one platoon from the medium machine gun battalion, 6th Battalion The Cheshire Regiment, and the fire support of a battery of 86th Field Regiment, Royal Artillery (The Hertfordshire Yeomanry).

The operational tasks confronting 6 Green Howards were not Hastings' only worries in the hectic weeks before D Day. Every day seemed to bring its own crop of complications. Though insignificant individually, when set against the sheer size of the proposed operation, each needed careful thought and resolution.

Among the 'imports' to 6 Green Howards was a large draft of Scotsmen, which included Lance Corporal Joyce, from Glasgow. Like others he went on a short spell of leave, to see his family and to release a little of the tension which months of hard training and the prospect of imminent action had built up. Unfortunately his relaxation went a little too far. Having

AVRE with fascine.

Flail tank clearing minefield.

The AVRE's 290 mm Petard mortar.

Armoured Vehicle Royal Engineers AVREs

imbibed rather too much of Scotland's national drink, and suffered from the effect which sudden fresh air has upon such a condition, he heaved a convenient brick through a near-by shop window and started to help himself to some of the contents. The Glasgow police were not amused and arrained him quickly before the local Sheriff who decreed that he should spend some time in prison. This worried Hastings. First, Joyce was an excellent soldier who would be much needed in Normandy. Secondly, and perhaps more alarmingly, if it became known that the best way to avoid taking part in a distinctly hazardous operation was to sling a brick through a shop window, there might not be many windows in Britain left unbroken. Hastings' powers of persuasion were tested to the full, but eventually a chastened Lance Corporal was released to go to Normandy. He was to prove his worth even before the Green Howards had cleared King Beach.

Another problem occurred when an RAF plane dropped a bomb squarely in the middle of the exit road which ran from the beach to the house with the circular drive. The aim might have been superb, but it was not appreciated by the Green Howards, for whom this road would be a crucial life-line up which the much-needed tanks, wheeled vehicles and supplies must follow them. However the planning experts seemed to have the answer to everything. Armed with dividers, graph paper and a recently taken air photograph, some genius worked out the width and depth of the hole. A fascine of the exact size was then constructed and placed on the top of an AVRE whose driver was told that once on the beach he was to drive up the road to the hole, dump his bundle in it and drive over it. In the event the measurements were perfect, the AVRE landed exactly at the right place, the driver placed his bundle squarely in the hole and trod it in. The axis road was open.

To his considerable frustration Hastings was not allowed to brief his men on the task confronting them. He would have liked at least to take his company commanders into his confidence, and they were obviously keen to know what was in store for them and their men. But the security instructions precluded this. He must keep his thoughts and fears to himself. If Hastings ever felt daunted by the task given him, he certainly never showed it. Under his leadership the battalion approached D Day in an atmosphere of the utmost confidence.

Impressed, like Peter Dickens, by the immense detail of his orders, Hastings was given little scope for his own inventiveness in planning the operation. The test for him and his subordinate commanders would come as the first soldiers waded ashore. It would be leadership, not planning, that would count when the Green Howards hit the beach. That in itself was a source of great comfort, for Hastings knew that he was backed by an experienced and reliable team, and the loyalty, courage and stubbornness in adversity of the Yorkshire soldier was almost legendary. Morale, leadership, confidence and the standard of training would be the cornerstones of success.

A few weeks before D Day the battalion moved south, first to

Lieutenant-Colonel Robin Hastings, Commanding Officer 6 Green Howards, briefs the master of the *Empire Lance* shortly before they sailed for D-Day.

Bournemouth and later to Winchester. Once there the gates of the camp were firmly shut. There would be no more leave; the time had come for the Yorkshiremen to be told the detail of their task. As they studied the photographs, models and maps that were now available, they, like others, were amazed by the detailed knowledge of the country over which they were about to fight and the thoroughness of the planning. Many hours were spent pouring over photographs, trying to pinpoint the beach defences and commit to memory all the key features which might be recognised when they emerged from their landing craft. The last few days of waiting passed quickly.

There are, of course, snags in even the best laid plans. Operation Overlord was no exception. Hastings and his battalion were to cross in the *Empire Lance*. This ship, which went by the name of a Landing Craft Infantry (LCI), was, in fact, a converted cargo ship, festooned with a mass of small landing craft into which the assaulting infantry would clamber for the final run-in to the beach. But once the Green Howards were aboard a staff officer went round the ship counting the number of landing craft, lifeboats and men. He then worked out that there was one too few lifeboats for the number of men on board, and declared that under no circumstances could the ship sail unless one of the landing craft was replaced by a lifeboat. As he watched his own battalion headquarters landing craft being removed, Hastings wondered momentarily whose side the man was really on. After weeks of training and rehearsals with the correct landing craft, he and his headquarters team must now go into the beach in one with which they had not practiced. It hardly seemed a good omen.

The first grey streaks of the dawn of 6 June were creeping into the eastern sky when Reveille was sounded in the Empire Lance. It was almost unnecessary; few had slept. Most had spent the time cleaning their weapons and making final checks of their equipment. Breakfast was unusually silent. The last meal before going into action is always difficult – the stomach feels tight and the appetite small. The next meal may be many hours away. For some there will be no next meal. A few natural humorists did their best to relax the atmosphere, but for the most part the Yorkshiremen picked at their food in silence, deep in their private thoughts. Fear of what the immediate future may hold; fear not so much of death but of the possibility of painful injury. Fear in anticipation is far worse than fear in the moment of action and danger. Once battle is joined events move far too quickly for most soldiers to be frightened. But the period of waiting beforehand seems interminable, and Operation Overlord, with its lengthy build-up and training, its final delay and its protracted Channel crossing, gnawed at the spirits of those involved.

Even hardened veterans, like Company Sergeant Major Stan Hollis of D Company, were glad when the time came to climb down the scrambling nets into the Landing Craft Assault (LCA) which would carry them ashore. The infantryman in his full assault equipment is a mass of buckles and buttons. All of these seemed to cling to the nets as if unwilling to leave the safety of the ship for the dangers and uncertainties that lay ahead. Weapons and equipment caught on the nets as they clambered down into the landing craft, which rose and fell alarmingly in the rough water. Hastings, normally a bad sailor, was surprised that he was not sea-sick on that rough journey; perhaps he had other things on his mind! On reaching the water Hasting's landing craft bucked violently in the swell, thereby making it almost impossible for the crew to detach the lowering hook, which weighed upwards of half a ton and which, when the craft was lifted on the high waves, bounced along the top of the battalion headquarters command carrier, at one end of which was a box of grenades and at the other the colonel's wash basin. Watching this Hastings felt ruefully that if the hook hit the grenades there would be no need for the wash basin! Eventually the hook was released and the landing craft took its place among the others circling round, waiting to line up for the

Infantry climb down the nets into a landing craft.

Running up towards the French coast and Gold Beach, camouflage covers have just been removed from this LCT at H-30. (Michael Irwin)

run in to the beach. After what seemed an age the time appointed came, and the vast armada of landing craft lined up and headed for the coast of Normandy.

It might be imagined that the first troops ashore in an invasion would be the leading infantrymen, but in this case it was not so. As the table on Page 29 shows the specialist armour, DD tanks, AVREs and Flails, would land first, to destroy previously identified defence strong-points and to clear exits through the minefields so that the assault infantry would not be pinned down on the beaches, unable to advance inland. (On Omaha Beach the Americans, with no armoured vehicles ashore in the early phases of the landings, suffered exactly this fate and many casualties.) Before the armour could go ashore, however, pathways must be cleared through the multitude of defence obstacles which, following Rommel's personal orders, now littered the beaches. This clearance was the task of the Landing Craft, Assault (Hedgerow) [LCA(HR)].

Lieutenant Michael Irwin RNVR commanded the nine LCA(HR) of Group 2, 591 Flotilla heading for King Beach. A veteran of landing craft, Irwin had taken part in the largely unopposed landings in North Africa in November 1942. At Salerno in Southern Italy in September 1943, however, it had been a very different story, as Irwin had had to land men from the 36(US) Division under heavy fire, straight into the teeth of strong German defences. It was an operation which nearly foundered. Now, for the third time, Irwin was leading a force towards an enemy-held beach.

Unlike the Infantry LCAs, which were transported across the Channel in large Landing Ships, to be launched a few miles out for the final run-in to the beach, the Hedgerows sailed the entire journey. They were to be towed most of the way by the Landing Craft Flak (LCF) and Landing Craft Tank (LCT). Cast off at 0615 about six miles out, they would then lead the way to the beaches. Once in position a few hundred yards off-shore, they would come into action. Welded to the deck of each Hedgerow were two banks, each of twelve 'mortar' barrels. Set into each barrel was a spigot, to the front end of which was attached a bomb containing 30 lbs of High Explosive, with a percussion cap on the end. Fired simultaneously at a range of between 335 and 415 yards, these 24 bombs would land among the beach obstacles and clear a lane 80 yards long by 12 yards wide. Following close behind the Hedgerows, the swimming DD tanks and the LCTs with the other specialist armour would then land. The armour would motor quickly through the cleared lanes onto the main beach area and start to neutralise the defences before the arrival of the first infantrymen a few minutes later. The landings were timed for shortly after low tide, when the beach obstacles would be clear of the water and therefore vulnerable to the Hedgehogs' attack. As soon as the lanes were cleared and marked,

Lieutenant Michael Irwin RNVR – 1944

A mountainous sea resulted in craft shipping vast amounts of water, and putting heavy strain on the tow lines. Seven of the nine LCAs in Group 2 broke their lines and had to make the journey under their own power. Here Irwin's coxwain concentrates on the job in hand. (Michael Irwin)

En route for France. Photo taken by Lieutenant Michael Irwin as his LCA (HR) 1110 is towed by LCF38. (Michael Irwin)

the follow-up landing craft, with the tide rising, would drive further up the beach with some degree of safety.

Battles seldom, if ever, run according to plan, and even this, the very first stage of the landings, with so much that must follow on that momentous day, ran into early troubles. The sea, on the night of 5/6 June 1944 was exceedingly rough, and the small LCAs, designed for work close in-shore not as cross-channel ferries, suffered accordingly. Bucking wildly in the mountainous sea they shipped vast amounts of water, and the pressure upon the tow lines from their tug Landing Craft proved to be too great. Seven of the nine LCAs in Group 2 broke their tow-lines and had to make the journey under their own power. Irwin's own LCA (HR) 1110 had to cast its tow at 0200 when its tug, LCF 38, broke down with engine trouble in mid-Channel. Eight of Irwin's LCAs made it to their appointed position on time – a remarkable feat of determination and seamanship.

As he closed in on his firing position, Irwin was conscious of an unnatural silence along the beach. The fire from the bombarding ships, which had been roaring over his head as he drove his craft shorewards, had momentarily lifted and there was as yet no response coming from the German defenders. Estimating his range at about 400 yards, Irwin ordered his two crewmen to take cover in the engine room as he operated the ripple switch which fired his banks of bombs. With a

Beach obstacles to be overcome by the invaders.

With the job done Irwin's LCA (HR) 1110 turns away from Gold Beach and heads back to parent ship *Empire Mace*. The two spigot mortar bombs, which failed to fire, can be clearly seen. (MICHAEL IRWIN)

satisfactory bang they flew towards the beach. Irwin just had time to notice that two had failed to fire, their firing mechanisms doubtless affected by the sea spray which had drenched the LCA during its journey. But conscious of LCT 930, with its load of Flail tanks, almost on top of him as its captain sought to follow up the Hedgerow's fire by landing his charges immediately after Irwin had cleared a path through the beach obstacles. Irwin just had time to order 'Hard a-port' as the bow of the LCT missed his craft by only a few feet.

Some were not so lucky. Sub Lieutenant Ashton's LCA(HR) 1106 was rammed and capsized by its following LCT just before it fired its spigot bombs. The LCA and two of the three crew members were lost.

Although Irwin's primary task was now over, he had one more duty to perform. Shortly before leaving England an Army officer had visited his LCA and delivered some sticky bombs. Having fired his spigot mortars, Irwin was to attach these sticky bombs to some of the beach obstacles. This would involve

manoeuvring the craft carefully alongside these fearsome looking objects, leaning over-board and pressing the sticky bomb against them. It promised to be a most unhealthy business, as the German defences would doubtless have come to life and be pouring fire along the beaches. Nor did it seem sensible to Irwin to introduce some new gadget, with which no-one had trained, just a few hours before departure. But orders were orders and having fired his main charges Irwin started to undertake this unpleasant task, as bullets from a German machine-gun whipped just over his head. His first few attempts all failed; the bombs refused to stick and fell into the water. Without further ado Irwin set sail for his parent ship, the *Empire Mace*, where his LCA was hoisted aboard. As he withdrew he could see the leading infantry-men storming up the beach, while the two Flails which had landed from LCT 930 just behind him were now both in flames. For most, D Day was just beginning; for Irwin it was over.

Of the eight LCA(HR) of Group 2 which reached the French coast five made it back to their parent ship. In addition to the one that was run over, two others foundered on their way to the *Empire Mace*, having completed their primary tasks – and had similarily unsuccessful experiences with the sticky bombs!

A Landing Craft Assault (LCA) carried twenty men and two Royal Marines – one to operate the engine, the other to open the front ramp for landing. From his LCA CSM Hollis of D Company, the left assault company of 6 Green Howards, could see A Company on his right and the 5 East Yorkshires on his left. About half a mile from the shore Hollis began to pick out the landmarks which he had learned so well from the air photographs and models back in England – the house with the

House with circular drive

Beach pillbox

King Beach, the exit road and the house with the circular drive. This photograph, taken from a low flying aircraft, was memorised by all members of 6 Green Howards.

circular drive, the road running up to it from the beach and an ominous-looking pill-box on the sea wall. It was clear that they would land dead on target, which was greatly reassuring. The operation ahead would be hard enough without the difficulty of landing off-target and having to re-cast the battalion operation while still on the beach. But Hollis was mesmerised by that pill-box. It was so sited that it could bring devastating fire along the beach. A man of action, as he was shortly and convincingly to prove, Hollis took a machine-gun from one of his soldiers, balanced it on the landing craft's ramp, and fired several bursts at the pill-box as it came within range. Perhaps that would daunt the ardour of any Germans inside. As they came in to land he grabbed the barrel and lifted the gun from the ramp, which would shortly go down, quite forgetting in the excitement of the moment that the barrel would be hot – he received a painful burn across the palm of the hand.

'A self-inflicted wound, quite the most painful I had the entire war, it took weeks to heal and the battle hadn't even started."

COMPANY SERGEANT MAJOR STAN HOLLIS VC

44

Ironically the 'pill-box' was nothing of the sort. A tramline used to run along behind the sea-wall, and this was just one of the shelters for waiting passengers. It still stands, and the marks of Hollis's shooting can still be seen.

Approach King Beach by the coast road, the D 514. Four and a half miles east of Arromanches, or three miles west of Corseulles, there is a small cross-roads. A track runs north down to the beach about 400 yards away. **Turn south** – there is a small sign, easily missed, saying 'Musée America Gold Beach'. After just fifty yards **turn right**, along Rue Claude Debussy, with a high wall on the left. A sign points to 'Residence Les Loges'. **Park** opposite the gateway in that wall and face the sea. You are looking down onto King Beach, where, at just after 0730 on the morning of 6 June 1944, 6th Battalion The Green Howards landed in France. In front is the track running up from the beach, through the gap in the hedge, joining the main road where you turned off. The wall behind you is that of 'The house with the circular drive', which was such a vital marker to the Green Howards. In 1944 it stood alone. Now it is seems almost lost among the new houses that have been built over the years.

The ramps went down and the Yorkshiremen piled out into the water which came up to their waists. Weighted down with equipment, some stumbled and fell before reaching the beach. Among them was Sergeant Hill, of 16 Platoon, who had been with D Company throughout the desert and Sicily campaigns, but who was tragically killed when he tripped on leaving the landing craft and was run over as it drove into the beach.

Infantry storm ashore from a landing craft.

Hollis, accompanied by three machine gunners and three mortarmen, raced up to the high-water mark where they were to lay down a smoke-screen to cover the German minefield as the rest of the company crossed it. It seemed almost unnecessary. From behind them the guns of the naval ships standing off the beaches and the artillery fire from guns on the approaching landing craft poured an incessant stream of fire onto the enemy positions. The smoke and dust of battle already shrouded the area. As he directed the fire of his small group Hollis saw a line of birds sitting quietly on the barbed wire just a few feet away, apparently quite unconcerned in the midst of all this fury. Private Mullally followed his sergeant major's gaze. 'No bloody wonder, sergeant major', was his dour comment, 'there's no bloody room for them in the air'.

Hastings landing craft followed close on the heels of those of his leading companies. The driver drove it hard into the beach where the nose stuck firmly. The tail then started to swing slowly round. Hastings watched with increasing alarm as it approached one of the German defensive beach obstacles – a mine attached to a pole. It was clear that in a very short time the rear of the landing craft would hit it. It was obviously sensible to disembark quickly. The drill was that immediately land was hit the ramp went down and the men on board leapt off and rushed up the beach. But this just did not happen. All sat firmly in their places, as if frozen solid, with the ramp still shut and no-one keen to open it, while the tail swung slowly but surely towards the mine. After what seemed an age, but was probably only a few seconds, one of the crew gave the ramp a shove. It went down to reveal a stretch of water between landing craft and land. Once again Hastings expected everyone to rush off up the beach, eager to release the tension and join the fray. But again, no-one moved. So, with an eye on the approaching mine, Hastings walked to the front of the craft, sat down on the edge and lowered his feet gingerly into the water in the manner of a Brighton paddler. The water just reached his ankles as he touched the bottom, so he thankfully rose and advanced up the beach without further ado, followed by the rest of his party.

On reaching the sea wall his first concern was to find out how his leading companies were progressing. He put up his binoculars but could see nothing. Looking down he saw that a bullet or mortar splinter must have snapped off the eye pieces.

Until that moment he had been totally unaware of the heavy firing which echoed along the entire beach.

On the right A Company was pinned down on the beach by heavy fire from a nearby pillbox and a German 105mm gun position. These problems were solved when a tank of B Squadron 4/7 DG, under command of 6 Green Howards, managed to 'post a letter' in through the firing slit of the 105mm gun emplacement, while Lance Corporal Joyce, who Hastings had saved from a Glasgow cell, now proved the accuracy of his throwing arm. Covered by Major Honeyman, his company commander, he jumped the sea wall, lobbed a grenade into the pillbox, and then followed it up quickly, rounding up the Germans who had survived. (L/Cpl Joyce was awarded the Military Medal for his actions on D Day.) The way was now clear for B and C Companies to pass through and advance towards the next objective, the Meuvaines Ridge.

On the left D Company, having successfully passed through the minefield and a gap in the hedge, was beginning to make its way up the road towards the house with the circular drive. Shortly after coming through the hedge they had their first battle casualties – from enemy fire in the area of the house. The leading two platoons pressed rapidly forward, bypassing the house, intent on reaching the Mont Fleury gun battery as quickly as possible. Company headquarters, with Major Ronnie Lofthouse and CSM Stan Hollis, followed up the road and approached the wall in front of the house. They had paused about fifty yards short of the gate when Lofthouse spotted the source of the fire, which had now been turned onto the back of the platoons which, having moved further inland, were now ahead about to start their assault on the gun battery.

'There's a pillbox in there, sergeant major,' he said, pointing to an area of bushes about fifty yards to the right, beyond the end of the wall. Hollis reacted instantly. Not waiting for orders he charged the pillbox alone, firing his Sten-gun as he ran. The Germans turned their fire on him as he raced towards them. Unaccountably, they missed. Within a few seconds he had reached the pillbox, shoved his gun muzzle in through the firing slit and sprayed it around like a hose-pipe. He then climbed on top of the pillbox, lay down and slipped a grenade in through the slit. When it exploded, with a satisfactory bang, he jumped down into the trench at the back which led to the entrance.

Bursting into the pillbox he found two dead Germans and a number of others who were either wounded or dazed – at least they clearly did not want to fight any more. Emerging from the pillbox, Hollis noticed that the trench led towards another pillbox about one hundred yards further on. If this was occupied by another group of Germans who might also shoot-up the platoons advancing on the Mont Fleury Battery, the advance might grind to a halt. He decided to investigate further on his own. Having changed the magazine on his Sten-gun, he started to walk along the trench. As he did so German soldiers started to emerge from the pillbox. But they seemed disinclined to tussle with Hollis, whose manner doubtless made clear to them the penalties of anything other than instant surrender. Prudently, they all put their hands up; in this way Hollis captured 25 to 30 prisoners, who he directed down towards the beach, where the beach group would doubtless look after them.

The leading platoons of D Company now nearing the battery were probably quite unaware of the drama behind them, but had the Germans been able to direct unsuppressed fire onto the rear of these platoons D Company's operations on D Day would probably have progressed no further.

Face the gate in the wall which leads to the house with the circular drive, with the sea behind you. **Turn right**. The road leads on towards some new houses. The second house on the right of the road has been built on the site of Hollis' first pillbox. The trench system has also been built over, but the concrete casemates of the Mont Fleury Gun Battery still exist, now incorporated into some of the gardens and sheds which have since sprung up in the area. They can be seen along the Rue de Roguettes in the village, just over the ridge.

As the morning passed Colonel Hastings was able, with considerable satisfaction, to tick off the various tasks he had been given. Beach, pillboxes and the house with the circular drive had all been captured. The garrison of the Mont Fleury Battery, after the hammering they had received from the air bombardment and naval guns, had decided that discretion was the better part of valour and had fled without a fight. B Company, under Major Young, had, despite an unexpected minefield, cleared its objective and taken more prisoners. C Company had linked up successfully with B Squadron 4/7DG

Exit road from King Beach, 1998, showing the house with the circular drive. It was just in front of the gate that Hollis became aware of the German pill-box. ○ marks where Hollis was when he saw the pillbox.

1998 the scene of the first part of Hollis' VC. The gate leading to the house with the circular drive is on the left.

and together they had captured the German position on the Meuvaines Ridge, which turned out to be, not a rocket site, but a command headquarters. From this position another 40 prisoners were making their way disconsolately down to the beach en route for prison camps in England.

Things were going far better than Hastings had ever dared to hope. But his natural satisfaction was tempered by one major worry. Although the overall casualty figures were not unexpectedly high, 6 Green Howards had lost too many key leaders. C Company commander, Captain Linn, had been killed during the attack on the Meuvaines Ridge, and the second-in-command, Captain Chambers, had been wounded in the head – fortunately not too badly as he was able to remain and assume command of the company. Major Jackson of Support Company had been seriously wounded on the beach. In addition several platoon commanders and non commissioned officers had been hit. Leadership by example had always been the battalion's creed, and this inevitably meant that the leaders were always at the most dangerous place – the front. Lieutenant Kirkpatrick of 16 Platoon D Company had been injured on the beach. He had fought throughout the morning with a broken arm. Now, on the advance forward from Mont Fleury, he too had been killed. This continual drain on the leadership of the battalion, if it persisted, would have an inevitable and adverse effect on the fighting quality of the battalion. But although Hastings was understandably concerned, he knew that other battalions were in greater difficulties, still fighting fierce battles on the beaches. He, at least, had secured room to manoeuvre. St Léger was still a long way further on. They must press on as quickly as possible.

The battalion advance from Mont Fleury along the road to Crépon was conducted under desultory German fire. B and C Companies led, with D tucked in behind and A in reserve. Just short of Crépon they came under withering fire from the village. Captain Jones, the much respected commander of the Carrier Platoon, was killed just short of the village. It was clear that the village was strongly held and that any further advance would be impossible unless the road through it was cleared. This road must become the battalion's lifeline as they advanced south. Along it must come the wheeled vehicles bringing food, ammunition and other vital stores. But Hastings did not want to

An aerial view of King Beach and the advance to the Mont Fleury gun battery, clearly still under construction at the time of this photograph. The effects of RAF bombing can be clearly seen.

KING BEACH

A COY

D COY

PILLBOX

HOLLIS

House with
circular
drive

PILLBOX

MT FLEURY BATTERY

MONT
FLEURY

get involved in a costly and time consuming street battle. He knew that his top priority was to press on as fast as possible towards his ultimate objective five miles further south.   He therefore ordered B and C Companies to bypass Crépon and push on; D Company must clear the route through the village. This would be something of a gamble. The opposition in Crépon might be more than D Company could deal with on its own, and he would only have A Company as a reserve, to help out both the leading companies and D Company. But to the experienced Hastings the risk was both carefully calculated and necessary.

He sent for Major Lofthouse and made it clear that the road must be opened, but that D Company must not get bogged down in trying to clear out every German from the village. They were to do just sufficient to ensure that the road was open for use. Lofthouse decided that the best he could do was to search the houses that actually overlooked the road. He collected his platoon commanders and gave them their orders. With Lieutenant Kirkpatrick killed as the company left the Mont Fleury area and Sergeant Hill killed on the beach, 16 Platoon had become leaderless. Lofthouse had therefore ordered his company sergeant major, CSM Stan Hollis, to assume command of the platoon.

To reach Cépon from King Beach, **follow the D112 inland** for two miles. En route, and just before leaving Ver-sur-Mer, you may be able to make out the faint invasion markings on a wall ahead as the road bends right – CREPON ASSEMBLY AREA - ALL DUMPS - Tɪ. (Tɪ denotes Tyne-Tees and was the tactical sign of 50th (Northumbrian) Division.) Since the war a bypass has been built around Crépon, passing it to the north. Stop, en route, to admire the splendid War Memorial dedicated to those of 6th and 7th Battalions The Green Howards who died during the Normandy campaign. Unveiled in 1996 by the regiment's Colonel-in-Chief, King Harald V of Norway, it takes the form of a splendid statue of a soldier, sitting at rest, but alert, before a wall on which are engraved the names of his fallen comrades. It is, perhaps, the most moving of all the many British memorials in Normandy, and is well worth visiting. About 100 yards beyond the memorial, **turn right**, still the D112, signed Bazenville and Bayeux. Go ¹/₂ mile to the last farm on the left, a large gate set in a high wall, almost opposite a Priority Road sign. This is Ferme du Pavillon, the home of the Lahaye family. Inside the farmyard, the farmhouse is immediately on your right and just beyond it a narrow alley, with a wall on the left,

Cromwell and Sherman tanks moving inland from King Beach towards the house with the circular drive.

King Beach and the exit road, 1998.

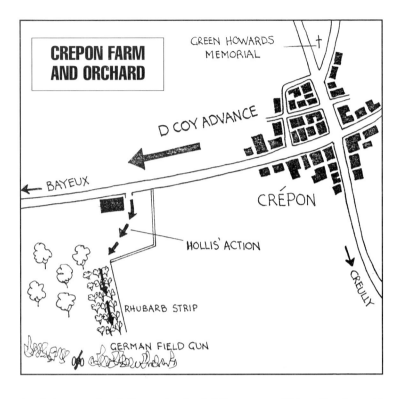

CREPON FARM AND ORCHARD

GREEN HOWARDS MEMORIAL

D COY ADVANCE

BAYEUX

CRÉPON

HOLLIS' ACTION

RHUBARB STRIP

GERMAN FIELD GUN

CREULLY

leads to an orchard. If you plan to visit the scene of this action it would only be reasonable to ask the permission of the family.

So far D Company's advance through the village had gone well. Now 16 Platoon must clear this farmhouse. Hollis led his men into the farmyard and quickly set about searching the house. He burst into one room and found a small boy of about ten cowering in the corner, clearly expecting to be shot. But Hollis, who must have presented a fearsome spectacle, just lowered his weapon and gave a toothy grin. (The boy, M Lahaye, later inherited the farm and greeted Hollis as a friend annually on British Army Battlefield Tours.) Satisfied that the rest of the house was empty, Hollis, being of an inquisitive nature, decided to look around the farm to ensure that there were no Germans concealed there. Cautiously he led his men down the narrow alley in the corner of the yard. Reaching the far end he peered gingerly round the corner. He hardly had time

PIAT anti-tank gun of the type used by CSM Hollis.

to absorb the detail of the orchards and fields when there was a sharp crack and a bullet gouged out a flake of the stone wall a few inches from his face. Hastily he withdrew, waited a few seconds and then, lying down this time, ventured another look. This time no bullet, just a scene of pastural tranquility – an orchard, a field surrounded by high hedges about 150 yards away and a couple of dogs jumping around wagging their tails near a gap in the hedge. A veteran of many battles, Hollis did not miss the significance of those dogs. Clearly there was someone, with whom the dogs were friendly, in the area of that gap. Hollis looked hard and could just make out what he thought was a field gun, concealed in the leafy hedge.

He hurried back to Lofthouse on the road and explained what he had seen. The company commander promptly authorised him to take a small party and try to eliminate the gun. So Hollis collected a PIAT anti-tank gun and rejoined his

Gateway into Ferme Du Pavillon, Crépon. Hollis found the small boy cowering inside the farmhouse on the right. The alley to the orchard is at the far end of the farmhouse.

CSM Stan Hollis went back for two of his men and at great personal risk extricated them from in front of a German gun position.

men in the farmyard. Quickly he gave out simple orders. He had earlier noticed that running down the left-hand side of the orchard towards the hedge was a strip of rhubarb about five yards wide. Hollis with his PIAT and two Bren-gunners would crawl down through the rhubarb in order to get closer to the field-gun, thereby giving a better chance of a hit with what was always a notoriously inaccurate weapon. At the same time several of his men were to dash out into the middle of the orchard and give covering fire for this hazardous operation.

Instructions clear, they set off. Hollis and his Bren-gunners started their tortuous crawl down the rhubarb strip, but there was no covering fire from the others; they had all been killed, by rifle and machine-gun fire from from a very alert enemy in the hedge, as soon as they broke cover into the open orchard. Hollis crawled on. Reaching the far end of the rhubarb he loaded his PIAT. Taking careful aim on the field gun, he fired. The round fell short. With horrible inevitability the gun traversed slowly until Hollis seemed to be gazing directly down its barrel at a range of only about one hundred yards. There was a shattering explosion. The shell passed over his head and slammed into the house behind him.

'To hell with this; I'm getting out of here,' was the way Hollis would later describe his reaction. Shouting to the two Bren-gunners to follow him, he started to crawl back through the rhubarb. Reaching the end he doubled down the narrow passage, rejoined the rest of D Company on the road and

HOLLIS FIRED HIS
PIAT FROM HERE

GERMAN GUN

RHUBARB PATCH

Orchard at Ferme Du Pavillon. The wall on the left is the end of the small alley.

Infantrymen of 50 Division moving inland past the village of Crépon, on the afternoon of D-Day.

Striking memorial to the Green Howards at Crépon.

reported to Lofthouse. The company commander was keen to press on quickly. He decided that as the field gun was not directly threatening the route through the village it should be left for others to sort out later.

But as Lofthouse and Hollis were talking they heard the sound of machine-gun fire from the area of the farmhouse. Hollis suddenly realised that the two Bren-gunners who had accompanied him had not returned. Since he had taken them in, he would get them out. Exchanging his PIAT for a Bren-gun he doubled back into the farmyard and down the narrow alley. On reaching the far end he charged straight into the middle of the orchard, firing from the hip and shouting to the two soldiers to get out. Totally disregarding the bullets flying around him, and standing beside the bodies of the soldiers who had died there earlier, he covered the withdrawal of his two Bren-gunners. As soon as they had reached the safety of the alley, by which time his magazine was empty, Hollis sprinted after them. Together the three men rejoined D Company on the road, miraculously unharmed.

6 Green Howards continued their advance until, by nightfall, they had reached a point just one mile short of their planned objective, the St Léger feature astride the Caen-Bayeux road. During D Day the battalion had about 90 casualties, which Colonel Hastings considered to be 'not unreasonable, bearing in mind the tasks given that day'. For his actions in clearing the pillbox at Mont Fleury and in the orchard at Crépon on D Day Company Sergeant Major S.E. Hollis was awarded the Victoria Cross, the only man to be so decorated on D Day. Lieutenant Colonel R.H.W.S. Hastings was also decorated for his leadership on D Day. He was awarded the first of his two DSOs, which he later described as 'quite undeserved personally, but probably par for the course for a battalion commander who survived D Day and whose battalion did quite well

CHAPTER FOUR

TANK ACTION AT CREULLY – PM D DAY

4th/7th Royal Dragoon Guards was an armoured
regiment in 8 Armoured Brigade. For the D Day landings
it was placed under command of 69 Infantry
Brigade, with a squadron allotted to each infantry
battalion. Initially the plan was for the regiment
to swim its tanks ashore. This highly unlikely
sounding performance for a 30-ton tank had
in fact been carefully thought out and prepared.
Each tank was fitted with a flotation screen and a
Duplex-Drive (DD) system which would propel it
through the water. On reaching land the flotation screens
would be lowered. Tanks being somewhat unnatural
swimmers, all crews were trained in submarine-escape
techniques. As D Day approached it was decided that while B
and C Squadrons would indeed swim ashore, landing five
minutes ahead of the two assault battalions, B Squadron with 6
Green Howards on the right of King Beach and C Squadron
with 5 East Yorkshires on the left, A Squadron's landing craft
would drive right onto the beach at H+45 minutes.

The removal of A Squadron's amphibious status and
equipment was largely to cater for the introduction of the 17-
pounder gun. It had already become apparent that the normal
75mm gun on the Sherman, excellent as it was for providing fire
support for attacking infantry, lacked the penetrative power to
knock out the German MkIV, Panther and Tiger tanks. Shortly
before D Day most armoured regiments were issued with a few
modified Shermans, with a new turret mounting a much more
powerful 17-pounder gun. This 'Firefly', as it was known, could
not be converted as a DD tank because the 17-pounder barrel
was too long to fit inside the raised flotation screen. In 4/7DG
the five Fireflies were given to A Squadron, whose landing-craft
must therefore be driven right onto the beach.

The men of A Squadron liked the Sherman tank. It was far
more comfortable and reliable than the old Valentine with
which they had trained until re-equipped in late 1943. It was not

An amphibious Sherman DD Tank, with flotation screen lowered. Its 75mm gun was no match for German tanks.

The Sherman 'Firefly'. Its 17 pounder gun, could knock out German tanks.

that Lieutenant Alastair Morrison, aged 20 and commanding 4th Troop of A Squadron, was over-concerned about comfort. This was to be his first taste of battle, but the training through which Major Jackie d'Avigdor-Goldsmid had put A Squadron in recent months had made it quite clear that war would be hard enough without the added disadvantage of having to fight in an uncomfortable tank.

Goldsmid, who had fought in France in 1940 and been evacuated from Dunkirk, had pushed his squadron hard. They had trained in all conditions – wet, dry, hot, cold, open country and built-up areas. They had spent many nights at sea, coming in at dawn to land and link up with the infantry. It had been Goldsmid's intention that there would only be one new problem to be faced when they landed in Normandy – the enemy.

Morrison's troop had three tanks. His own and Corporal Johnson's had the 75mm gun. The anti-tank punch for 4th Troop was provided by Sergeant Harris' Firefly, with the more lethal 17-pounder gun. But with its longer gun barrel and different turret, the 'Firefly' would be an obvious target for the German gunners. For the most part, therefore, Morrison and Johnson led in the 75mm tanks, with Harris' tank tucked in behind to cover them forward and move quickly to engage enemy tanks, when a particular threat developed.

The final loading onto the invasion landing craft went like clockwork. To Morrison it all seemed exactly like an exercise. When loaded the craft collected together in groups of four, hidden under voluminous camouflage nets. Shortly after they had tied up, as Morrison was idly watching the mass of small boats which buzzed around the invasion fleet, he was surprised to see a Royal Engineer motor barge come alongside, bringing an officer, fifteen sappers and a vast 5-ton coil of beach matting. As the sappers worked feverishly at welding this contraption onto the landing craft just behind the ramp, the officer collected all the tank crews together.

'This,' he said, 'is the Roly-Poly Beach-Mat. As soon as the landing craft hits the beach and the ramp goes down, two men are to run forward and unroll the mat up the beach. The tanks will then drive along the mat.' And, with that rather terse instruction, he left.

The tank crews of 4th Troop were sceptical. Having rehearsed the landings many times, they knew exactly what to do. Why

Major Jackie d'Avigdor-Goldsmid (in steel helmet) commanding a Guard of Honour for a famous visitor to 4/7 Dragoon Guards prior to leaving for France.

introduce some new, unproven gadget at this last minute? Their concern was clearly shared by the rest of A Squadron, because late that night the troopers set about the beach-mat. After a brief resistance it disappeared overboard with a huge splash, to cheers from the soldiers.

4/7DG's experiences of the crossing to France were much as others. However, as they neared the coast the local Naval Commander decided that the sea was too rough to launch the DD tanks for their swim into the beach. He would bring them into a deep-wade, just a few hundred yards short of the beach. This proved to be a very wise decision. Whereas all the tanks launched at the US Omaha Beach sunk in the long swim in to the beach, B and C Squadrons of 4/7DG reached Gold Beach with only a few tank casualties.

Behind the leading squadrons, A Squadron arrived at about 8.30, accompanying the reserve infantry battalion, 7 Green Howards. The landing went largely according to plan, with the exception of the loss of two tanks which fell into underwater shell holes and were swamped. There was a short delay while the German minefield was breached, and then A Squadron and 7 Green Howards set off along the main axis, past Crépon towards Creully, a small village about five miles inland. As they advanced with 1st and 3rd Troops leading, and the infantry riding on the backs of 2nd and 4th Troops behind, they encountered little significant opposition. Occasionally a pair of hands would protrude above the corn, to be followed by a German soldier who, obedient to the signals of the passing troopers, made his way disconsolately north towards the beach. In an orchard just south of Ver-sur-Mer they paused only briefly to dump the supplies of extra ammunition which they had brought over, and which was to be the regiment's immediate reserve. Then on, as quickly as possible, towards Creully.

The bridge at Creully was important. The River Seulles wanders from west to east across the countryside. Pre-invasion intelligence had reported that it was likely to prove a tank obstacle. Goldsmid had realised the significance of this bridge and had determined to seize it intact as quickly as possible. The leading tanks were about to cross the main road just north of Creully when a German staff car, driven at great speed from west to east, came into view. It was quickly engaged by machine-gun fire and slithered into the ditch. Inside was a dead

German Medical Colonel. The squadron moved quickly on. 2nd Troop, which Goldsmid had ordered to take the lead, crossed the main road and started to make its way down the narrow winding road towards the Creully bridge.There was an early scare when it was reported that there was a Panther tank on the bridge, but it quickly withdrew and A Squadron was able to motor over the bridge in single file, and climb the hill, under the over-hanging walls of the old Norman castle, into the middle of the village. The tank crews were conscious of a feeling of vulnerability as they drove past houses which seemed to crowd in upon them, each a potential haven for a German sniper who could so easily pick off the tank commanders, with their heads out of their tank turrets. One shot from a German anti-tank weapon at very short range in that narrow street would have destroyed the leading tank, thereby blocking the entire advance.

It was with a distinct sense of relief that the squadron emerged from the village and into open country. They passed through a line of trees just south of the village and surveyed the scene ahead.

The small town of Creully lies just south of the D 12, the main road from Courseulles to Bayeux, about 5 miles from the coast and 7 miles from Bayeux. From the Ferme du Pavillon (Chapter 3) **return** the ½mile to the cross roads in Crépon. **Turn right** (south) onto D 65, following signs to Creully. After crossing the D 12 (1½ miles), the road bends downhill to the water-meadows of the River Seulles. Ahead, on the high ground, is Creully, with its imposing castle. Just after **crossing the river**, pull in on the left and admire the War Memorial of 4th/7th Royal Dragoon Guards, unveiled in 1992 by their Colonel-in-Chief, the Duchess of Kent. Look back, over the river, towards the Chateau de Creullet. It was there that General Montgomery established his headquarters when he landed on 8 June, and it was from there that he conducted the Normandy Campaign.

Follow the road up the hill, under the almost over-hanging walls of the castle, to the road junction in the town centre, beside the French War Memorial. **Keep right**, on the D 35, signed to St Gabriel-Brécy. After ½ mile **turn left** onto the D 82, signed to Rucqueville and Coulombs. Drive past the industrial complex and stop at the far end of the electricity sub-station, where you can see the country for about a mile ahead.

It was a perfect summer day. The sun shone brightly in the

clear blue sky. A gentle breeze rustled the leaves of the trees and sent ripples through the corn, which was beginning to turn from the green of spring to the gold of mid-summer. In short it was a scene of undisturbed peace which confronted the men of A Squadron as they emerged from Creully – very different from the picture of war which Goldsmid had so graphically painted for them during training. Goldsmid's heart soared. This was good tank country – long fields of view but with folds in the ground and the occasional hedges and strips of wood which the squadron could use as tactical bounds as it advanced south. Here, for the first time since they had landed some hours earlier, he could deploy his squadron properly and press on at speed. The confined fields and hamlets were, for the moment at least, behind them. He pressed the transmit button on his radio and gave orders to his four troops:

'Shake out into two-up formation – 1st Troop left, 2nd right,
3rd and 4th behind 1st and 2nd respectively. Now let's go.'

Morrison caught the confident ring in his squadron leader's voice. He manoeuvred his three tanks into their appointed place behind 2nd Troop, and watched the leading tanks, with Squadron Headquarters between and just behind them, as they disappeared over a gentle crest about 200 yards ahead. Near the front of the advance Goldsmid's practiced eye noted every detail of the countryside.Things might be fine for the moment, but he well knew that it could all change very rapidly. Where was the most likely hiding place for an enemy anti-tank gun? Where was the nearest cover into which the squadron could move if it suddenly came under fire. To the right the ground seemed to fall away towards the River Seulles. Tanks could easily use the contours of the ground to gain protection on that side. On the more exposed left there was a belt of trees about 400 yards ahead.

Then quite suddenly two tanks to his right seemed to explode in sheets of flame, followed quickly by clouds of dense smoke. In a quick glance he saw that they were those of Sergeant Partlow and Corporal Lipscombe of 2nd Troop. Goldsmid had heard nothing above the noise of his tank engine and the crackle of his radio. Nor had he seen anything. But he knew that the leading tanks were in open country and probably exposed to a very alert and accurate German gunner.

'Speed up. Make for cover - the line of trees 400 yards ahead.'

Lieutenant Peter Aizlewood with 1st Troop was already nearing the line of the trees, watching intently to see if he could locate the German tank or anti-tank gun which had struck so suddenly. Squadron Headquarters and Lieutenant Charles Pillman's 3rd Troop hastily joined them. On the right the remaining tank of 2nd Troop, that of the troop leader Lieutenant Michael Trasenster, had prudently withdrawn a little, using a fold in the ground to conceal it from enemy fire.

Behind, Morrison had seen none of this. The first hint of trouble had come from hearing the hurried orders from his squadron leader. He had as yet no idea what had caused them. Tucked into the low ground to the right of the road, unable to see the leading tanks, Morrison felt somewhat cut off from events. Slowly he inched his way forward to where he could take in the detail of the scene. Ahead and to the right he could see the burning tanks of 2nd Troop, in the middle of the field. Over to the left 1st and 3rd Troops and Squadron Headquarters had now reached the line of trees. Morrison watched through his binoculars as one of the tanks nosed its way through the trees. Suddenly chunks of metal flew off the turret. Immediately a near solid column of dense black smoke spiralled vertically upwards for about 100 feet.

Morrison was surprised. Throughout their training he had formed a mental picture of a tank 'brewing-up'. He had expected to see a few sparse flames lick from the stricken tank, to be followed by the hurried disembarkation of the crew, possibly wounded or burned, and shortly after by the thud of ammunition exploding inside. But reality was quite different. The tank had suddenly become an instant inferno. And to his right he could see that the turret of one of 2nd Troop's tanks was glowing red. Above both tanks a black pillar of smoke hung as if suspended from some invisible beam.

Morrison was now in something of a quandary. Ahead of him, 2nd Troop, down to just the troop leader's tank, was clearly stuck, unable to push forward on the right. The squadron radio net was momentarily silent – perhaps the tank which he had just seen hit was that of his squadron leader, Goldsmid. But there seemed little point in just sitting doing nothing, waiting for orders which might never come. He decided to join 1st and 3rd Troops in the line of trees. He gave orders to his driver, Corporal Gardner, and the tank set off at top

Effect of a direct hit on a Sherman. The Germans referred to it as the 'Tommy Cooker' because of its tendency to burst into flames on being hit.

speed across the open ground towards the trees.

'Hello 4 Able for 4 – I'd watch it if I was you.' The warning voice of Sergeant Harris crackled in his ear. But Morrison had calculated the risk – if he drove fast enough the German gunner, however alert and accurate, would be unlikely to be able to hit him. The tank bucked violently as it roared across the open field.

Reaching the tree line without mishap, Morrison breathed a sigh of relief and took stock of the situation around him. On the right was Pillman and 3rd Troop. Ahead, in a small clump of trees he could see 1st Troop, with Aizlewood's tank a little forward of the others in what looked like a good firing position. Morrison focused his binoculars on Aizlewood's tank. He wondered if the crew had yet been able to locate the enemy gunner. But as he watched he saw a spark, as if someone had struck a match against the side of Aizlewood's tank. Then 'woomph' from inside the tank and immediately the tell-tale column of black smoke erupted into the sky. Just one figure clambered out of the turret and fell into the corn.

By chance, directly over the top of Aizlewood's tank, Morrison had noticed a distinct flash at the foot of a telegraph

67

pole on a distant feature. That flash had been followed by a whisp of smoke which drifted away down a nearby hedgerow.

From where he was Morrison knew that he could not engage the target with direct fire. The brow of the hill in front of him prevented this. And the danger of going forward from his turret-down position was clearly indicated by the now-burning tank ahead. Any movement forward would expose his tank to fire from an alert and accurate enemy. The only answer must be an indirect shoot, with the gunner, unable to see the target, being given corrections by Morrison following the fall of each shot.

But herein lay a problem. While Morrison was justly proud of 4th Troop's ability to hit targets they could see, he had to admit that they had never shone at indirect shooting. This entailed a mass of mumbo-jumbo about 'bracketing' – the art of landing one shot beyond and one shot short of the target, then halving the bracket, and repeating the process until you hit it. In theory it all sounded so simple. There was, however, one snag – the commander must see the fall of shot if he was to send the necessary corrections. As far as 4th Troop was concerned the very mention of the words 'indirect shoot' seemed to activate some hidden gremlin. The gun would then take charge and despatch its shells into the far distance, never to be seen again. Corrections, of course, were then impossible.

But there was clearly no other option. With a slight sense of the inevitable Morrison gave orders to his crew. He gave a quick and rough estimate of the range, traversed the gun onto line and gave the order 'Fire'. There was a loud bang and Morrison almost hopelessly scanned the far horizon through his binoculars. In keeping with tradition, he saw nothing. He shortened the range and called for another round. To his utter astonishment, and for the first time ever, he saw the shell strike the ground some way short of the target. He halved the bracket, ordered another round and was both amazed and elated to see a sudden belch of flame and smoke in the area of the target.

'On target, three rounds gunfire.' The gunner, Trooper Hilliard, kept his foot on the firing button while the loader, Corporal Arnold, slammed the rounds successively into the breech of the gun.

As Morrison watched what he thought was the end of an enemy anti-tank gun he was conscious of a distinst feeling of pleasure. But not for long. Suddenly the entire area around him seemed to erupt with bursting shells. Not having been under heavy fire before, he found the experience not a little alarming. He was wondering where the fire was coming from when there was a voice in his earphones.

'What the hell do you reckon this is, sir?' It was Corporal Gardner, the driver, speaking on the intercom.

'Oh, I don't know.' Morrison tried to sound relaxed since he had absolutely no idea. 'Enemy mortar or something, I expect.'

At that moment a shell landed just beside the tank with a huge explosion, which shook the tank and covered it in a shower of dirt. A piece of shrapnel struck the side, which resounded like a deafening gong.

'Bloody heavy mortar!' growled Gardner from the bowels of the tank.

Aizlewood had not been in his tank when it was destroyed. He had dismounted and crawled forward to a small ridge to get a better view of the country and see whether he could pinpoint the German gunner. He was returning to his tank when it was hit. Of his crew of four, three were killed and the fourth wounded. Disconsolately he had walked over to his squadron leader's tank. It was while he was discussing with Goldsmid and Pillman what to do next that the shellfire suddenly burst all round them.

Morrison, at least, was in the comparative safety of his tank; only a direct hit would knock it out. But Goldsmid and his two troop leaders were unprotected, in the open, exposed to the fire. Quickly he told them to take cover, and then climbed back into his own tank while Aizlewood and Pillman sprinted towards Pillman's tank. They never made it. A shell landed on top of them as they ran. Pillman was killed instantly and Aizlewood so bady wounded that he was later to lose a leg.

Goldsmid was puzzled; it seemed to him that the fire was coming from behind them. Fortunately it ceased as abruptly as it had started, but not before 7 Green Howards, the infantry battalion with which A Squadron were operating, had suffered many casualties, having been caught in the open. Sadly Goldsmid was right; the fire had indeed come from behind. An inquiry later showed that someone ashore had called for fire support. The request had been passed up the Army channels to the Naval HQ Ship, which allocated HMS *Orion*, a cruiser with

69

'Enemy tanks destroyed – well done!' HMS *Orion's* 6-inch guns caused severe casualties to A Sqn 4/7 DG and the infantry. An example of excellent shooting but tragically poor target identification.

6-inch guns, and put her in touch with a spotter aircraft. *Orion's* log clearly records all the details, salvo by salvo, ending on a triumphant note 'Enemy tanks destroyed – well done'.

Lieutenant-Colonel Rodney Byron, commanding officer of 4/7 DG, decided that as they were only about a mile and a half short of what had always seemed to be a most optimistic objective, the advance should halt and they should sort out their casualties. A Squadron was to stay with the infantrymen until dark and then pull back into leaguer for the night.

Morrison heard Goldsmid's radio order that the squadron should withdraw a short distance to better and more secure positions. As he moved back towards the low ground nearer the river, the ground became steeper and the surface, now pock-marked with shell-holes, very uneven. But the high corn concealed the dips and hollows. Suddenly one of his tracks slipped into a hidden hollow and the tank rolled over on its side. Only a little shaken, Morrison crawled out of the turret and was reassured to see an American Thunderbolt aircraft circling overhead. With a bit of luck he would see the yellow recognition panel behind the turret and would protect the tank from enemy interference. This comforting thought was rudely interrupted when he realised that the aircraft was diving straight for him. What followed was exactly as it appears in films – sparks from the wings, a rattle of machine-gun fire and a furrow of earth ploughed up a few yards away from the side of the tank.

Morrison squirmed quickly back into the turret, seized an orange smoke grenade and lobbed it into the corn. Anxiously he watched to see whether the smoke would develop in time to inform the pilot of his mistake. It didn't; the second pass was

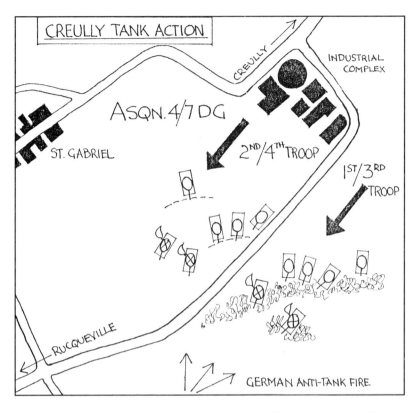

CREULLY TANK ACTION

CREULLY

INDUSTRIAL COMPLEX

ASQN. 4/7 DG

ST. GABRIEL

2ND/4TH TROOP

1ST/3RD TROOP

RUCQUEVILLE

GERMAN ANTI-TANK FIRE

correct for line but wrong for elevation. This time the bullets went a few feet over his head.

By now the orange smoke was billowing up into the sky. On his third run the pilot waggled his wings and disappeared over the horizon. Morrison breathed a sigh of relief that at least there was one pilot who was not a very good shot. To have been killed on D Day by an American fighter would indeed have been ironic.

As darkness approached and A Squadron prepared to withdraw into leaguer, to rearm and refuel for the next day's operations, Morrison decided to use the cover of darkness to recover his tank. He and Gardner went back to guide forward a recovery vehicle, leaving Hilliard and Lance Corporal Carter, the hull gunner, crouching in a hedge beside the tank. As dusk gathered Hilliard and Carter dimly saw two figures approaching the tank. 'Hardly likely to be a German patrol and

Lieutenant Alastair Morrison

certainly not one of ours', thought Hilliard. The only reasonable explanation seemed to be a couple of local farmhands on the lookout for a bit of loot. He decided to move them on quickly and fired a burst from his Sten-gun over their heads. This had the desired effect as the two figures ran away at speed, encouraged by another over-head burst. (Some twenty-one years later Goldsmid and Morrison returned to the area on one of their annual Battlefield Tours. They decided to visit the farm a few hundred yards ahead. Over a glass of Calvados the local farmer explained how he had helped the Allies during the invasion. The only unfortunate experience had been on D Day itself, when he and his son went out at dusk to help the crew of a British tank which had turned over in a nearby field. But their efforts had not been welcomed by the British soldiers, who had chased them off by firing a machine-gun at them, nearly killing them. Morrison decided not to reveal his part in the story!)

Like other commanders, Goldsmid took stock of the situation at the end of D Day. He remembered his thoughts of just eighteen hours earlier – the mixed emotions of expectation and anticipation. He remembered, too, the sense of history in the making as the tracks of his tank first gained purchase on the sand of Normandy. Now A Squadron was over five miles inland, within a very short distance of its final objective, and it had been responsible for the capture of a considerable number of prisoners and the destruction of several anti-tank guns. Against this had to be set the loss of seven killed, four injured and four tanks destroyed. The casualties would be a bitter blow to a squadron which had lived and trained together for many months. The whole had become a close-knit team, with each man trusting, respecting and relying upon the others. Now some were gone. But without being in any way complacent Goldsmid, as he walked round talking to the tank crews as they replenished their tanks, was fully aware that A Squadron's experience of D-Day could have been much worse, and that his hitherto unproven squadron had performed splendidly in its first battle.

CHAPTER FIVE

THE GERMANS REACT

By the end of D Day it was clear that the landings had succeeded. Even at Omaha, where the Americans had fought desparately all day to get off the beach, the foothold now seemed secure. Phase 1 of the Battle of Normandy had worked. Phase 2, the expansion of the beach-head and the build-up of forces ready for Phase 3, the break-out, must now begin. Between 6 June and 25 July, when General Bradley's 1st (US) Army broke-out in the west near St Lô, lay seven weeks of hard and bitter fighting.

Early on 8 June General Montgomery landed in Normandy, established his Headquarters at the Château de Creullet just north of Creully, and took stock. Caen, which had been a D Day objective of 3 British Division, was still firmly in German hands. It was clear from the actions of 21 Panzer Division that they did not intend to give it up without a stiff fight. That evening Montgomery wrote to General Simpson at the War Office in London:

> 'The Germans are doing everything they can to hold on to Caen. I have decided not to have a lot of casualties butting up

General Montgomery landing in Normandy 8 June 1944.

against the place.I have ordered 2nd Army to keep up a good pressure and to make its main effort towards Villers-Bocage and Evrecy, and thence south-east towards Falaise.'

He therefore decided to try to outflank Caen and secure the high, open ground astride the Caen-Falaise road to the south. If this could be achieved it would isolate the Germans defending Caen, which should then fall with out the need for a costly street-battle. There would be two additional advantages. First, it would allow room for General Dempsey's 2nd (British) Army to loose its armoured divisions into country that was far more suitable for tanks than the close country of the 'bocage', west of Caen. Secondly, it would give much needed space for the 2nd Allied Tactical Air Force to deploy its fighter and fighter-bomber squadrons on French soil, thereby ensuring far closer mastery of the airspace over the Normandy battlefield.

In outline Montgomery and Dempsey planned a pincer movement round Caen, using three of Montgomery's favourite divisions – all veterans of his 8th Army victories in the North African desert. On the right 7 Armoured and 50 Infantry Divisions would advance on Tilly-sur-Seulles and Villers-Bocage.On the left 51 (Highland) Division would move into 6 Airborne Division's bridgehead east of the Orne and then attack south, via Cagny, towards the high ground and Falaise. When

German troops move up through the ruins of Caen.

success from these two arms of the pincer seemed likely 1 Airborne Division would be flown from England and dropped deep beyond Caen, probably in the area of Mt Pincon, south of Villers-Bocage. To Montgomery's intense rage, this part of the plan was vetoed by Air Chief Marshal Leigh-Mallory, whose gloom about the chances of success matched his earlier, misplaced pessimism over the planned use of the airborne divisions on D Day. The concept was clear; its success depended in no small part upon the speed with which the Germans could bring their panzer divisions into the Normandy battle.

The Germans got off to a bad start on D Day. They had been taken completely by surprise when a message calling the French Resistance to arms at midnight was intercepted and decoded just after 2100 on 5 June. By 2230 Army Groups B and G and the Third Air Fleet had been put on alert. But many of the senior commanders who might have been able to influence the battle in the early stages in Normandy were away from their headquarters that night. Rommel, on a visit to Hitler to argue the case for strengthening the defences of the West Wall, had taken a day off to visit Ulm in Southern Germany for his wife's birthday on, of all days, Tuesday 6 June. General Dollmann, commander of 7th Army, had ordered General Meindl of 2nd Parachute Corps to conduct a Study Day on 6 June for all available senior commanders at his headquarters at Rennes in Brittany; the subject, ironically, – 'defence against the airborne and seaborne invasion of the Cotentin peninsula'. Dollmann himself and many of the Normandy divisional commanders were in Rennes. General Marcks, whose 84 Corps was responsible for the defence of Normandy and Brittany, had used the excuse of his birthday to be absent, while General Dietrich of 1 SS Panzer Corps was in Brussels.

There were three German panzer divisions in Normandy on D Day - 21, 12 SS and Panzer Lehr. Although splendid fighting formations, the command structure for tasking them was most unsatisfactory. Disagreement, between Field Marshal von Rundstedt and General Geyr von Schweppenberg on the one hand and Field Marshal Rommel on the other, about the use of these divisions, had led to the worst sort of command compromise. Rommel had insisted that the tanks should be under his command and deployed well forward where they

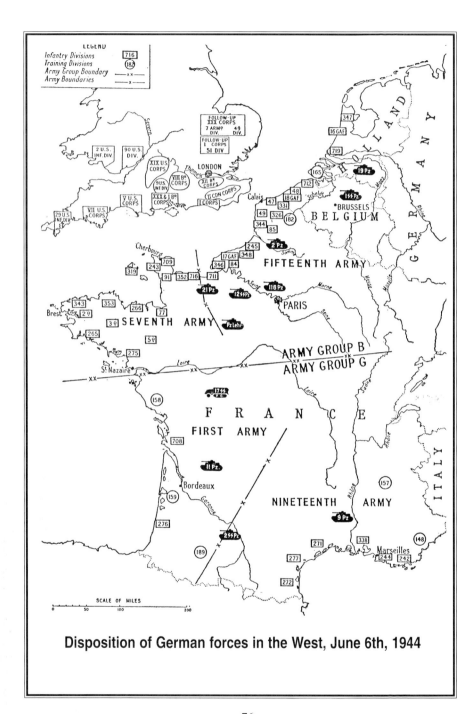

Disposition of German forces in the West, June 6th, 1944

could sweep the invasion forces back into the sea before the Allies could establish a firm footing. Von Schweppenberg, with von Rundstedt's backing, held the view that it would be foolish to commit the tanks before the main invasion point had been clearly identified. But from his desert experience Rommel knew that, with the Allies likely to have air supremacy, any formations moving forward towards the coast would be delayed and seriously written down by very heavy air attack. It is likely, however, that there was more to the disagreement than just a difference in tactical philosophy. By this stage in the war all those who now held senior commands were strong personalities; none would welcome handing over elements of his command to another. Von Schweppenberg's Panzer Group West, though deployed in Normandy, was not under the nominated command of Rommel. But von Schweppenberg himself had no operational command respons-ibility. He was responsible only for the administration and training of the panzer divisions. However, he hoped and expected that once hostilities broke out he would be given operational command of them. Conversely, Rommel insisted that once the invasion had been identified the three panzer divisions should immediately pass to his command; without their instant avail-ability he could not hope to defeat the invasion quickly. Von Schweppenberg, whose aristocratic background differed so much from that of Rommel, must have felt that to

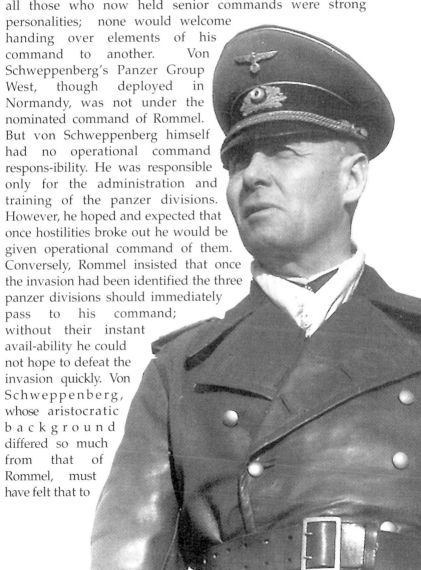

Colonel Meyer ('Panzer-Meyer') [left] Briefing Field Marshal von Rundstedt. Between is General Fritz Witt, Commander of 12 SS Panzer Division (Hitler Jugend) who was killed 14 June.

lose his panzer divisions at the moment that they became the key to victory or defeat was more than he could accept without a hard fight to retain them.

Von Rundstedt, a Prussian of the old school, and, at 69, some sixteen years older than his fellow Field Marshal, cannot have found Rommel an easy subordinate. Rommel's ambition, charisma, restless energy, coupled with his tactical flair and courage (he had won the Pour Le Mérite – the German equivalent of the Victoria Cross – as a junior officer in World War I) and his personal standing with and access to Hitler behind von Rundstedt's back, must have been very difficult for the elderly Field Marshal to accept. He could more easily identify with the conventional von Schweppenberg, who did not hide his dislike and jealousy of Rommel. The argument over command of the panzer divisions was taken to Hitler, whose compromise provided the worst possible solution. 21 Panzer Division would come under Rommel's command; the others were not to be deployed without Hitler's personal authority. And on the early morning of 6 June 1944 no-one was brave enough to disturb the Führer's sleep to seek their rapid deployment. By late afternoon, when authority was given, it was already too late; any chance of successfully opposing the invasion had gone. Only 21 Panzer Division was released for operations in the Caen area on D Day – and it was in the Caen area that the British achievements fell well short of expectations.

Although Rommel was undoubtedly tactically correct in his argument, it is highly unlikely that even if he had had command of the panzer divisions he could have thrown them into the battle for the beaches early enough to affect the outcome. Such was the Allied air forces mastery of the skies on the morning of D Day that 12 SS and Panzer Lehr Divisions would never have been able to get forward in daylight unimpeded. And by nightfall on D Day it would have been too late.

On 6 June 12 SS Panzer Division (*Hitlerjugend*), which was to acquire a fearsome reputation during the Normandy campaign, was stationed near Lisieux, about 25 miles east of Caen. At 1700 General Fritz Witt was ordered to move the division to the area of Carpiquet, just west of Caen, and there to mount counter-attacks against the Allied landings. The division moved overnight. By dawn on 7 June the leading elements, 25 SS Panzer Grenadier Regiment commanded by Colonel Kurt Meyer (well-known as Panzer-Meyer he was to take command of 12 SS when Witt was killed on 14 June) had arrived in the area, to be joined later that morning by a battalion of MkIV tanks from 12 SS Panzer Regiment. Throughout the rest of the day they attacked the Canadians advancing on Carpiquet, capturing Franqueville, Authie and Buron. Next morning more of the division arrived and was quickly thrown into the battle. 26 SS Panzer Grenadier Regiment occupied Audrieu, Cristot and Bruay. But between these two Panzer Grenadier regiments, 3 Canadian Division held a strong position based on Puttot-en-Bessin, Norrey-en-Bessin, Bretteville-L'Orgueilleuse and Rots. Late on 8 June the Germans attacked again. Panzer-Meyer, as ever at the head of his regiment, broke through Rots and managed to penetrate the Canadian position at Bretteville, but the defence held. After heavy fighting and many casualties on both sides, Meyer was forced to withdraw to the high ground east of Rots. Bretteville and Norrey remained firmly in Canadian hands.

By now the leading elements of General Fritz Bayerlein's Panzer Lehr Division, which had been ordered forward from its location near Chartres, was arriving in the area of Tilly-sur-Seulles. It, too, was quickly sucked into the battle. Early next morning, 9 June, Bayerlein led Panzer Lehr in a left-hook attack on Bayeux. By mid morning they had reached Ellon, just 3 miles south of the town, and Major Prince William von Schönberg-Waldenberg, commanding the tanks of 2nd Battalion Panzer Lehr Regiment, felt confident that, despite heavy Allied artillery and naval gunfire, he could easily and quickly secure the city. He was not pleased, therefore, to be ordered to pull back to Tilly. British pressure in the Audrieu and St Pierre area had threatened to drive a dangerous wedge between 12 SS and Panzer Lehr.

On the same morning Geyr von Schweppenberg, who had arrived from Paris and whose Panzer Group West had just been given operational responsibility for the Caen sector, visited the headquarters of 12 SS Division in the Abbaye d'Ardenne, just west of Caen. He was determined to co-ordinate the operations of the three panzer divisions in a concerted tank offensive aimed at driving 2nd British Army into the sea.

In the east 21 Panzer was to counter-attack the British advancing on Caen. On their left 12 SS would drive north-west into the Canadians, while Panzer Lehr would attack the British at Bayeux. But by coincidence the British were, at the same time, planning to launch their own pincer attacks. The result was several days of confused but fierce fighting. In the east, astride the River Orne and Caen Canal, 21 Panzer's attack encountered 3 and 51 (Highland) Divisions trying to advance south. In the centre 12 SS met the Canadians along the Caen-Bayeux road. Further west and just north of Tilly-sur-Seulles, Panzer Lehr found itself faced by the newly arrived 7 Armoured Division, which had been ordered to advance from the Bayeux area, take Tilly and press on to Villers-Bocage. Von Schweppenberg's plan for a concerted attack never materialised. Indeed all attempts by the Germans to co-ordinate their tanks into a major offensive failed. Constant pressure by the British and Canadians around Caen throughout June and July forced them into using their

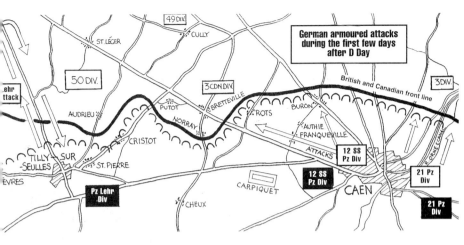

German armoured attacks during the first few days after D Day

British and Canadian front line

panzer divisions piecemeal, to bolster a defence which, like a rusty bucket, seemed to spring a new leak whenever the previous one had been plugged.

Slowly and remorselessly the British and Canadians extended their beach-head, disputed every yard of the way by dogged German defence. Casualties on both sides were high. And things were made even harder for the Germans when on 11 June, pinpointed by Ultra intercept, von Schweppenberg's Headquarters was bombed, most of his staff killed or wounded (von Schweppenberg himself was among the wounded) and much of the equipment necessary to effect command of the battlefield was destroyed. Little attempt had been made to conceal the headquarters from the air – clearly von Schweppenberg had still disregarded Rommel's advice about the effect of Allied air supremacy. Next day, 12 June, General Marcks, the impressive and much respected commander of 84 Corps, responsible for the defence of Normandy and Brittany, was killed in an air attack. It was hardly surprising that the German command structure faltered at this crucial period, and it was to be a further two vital weeks before Panzer Group West was to be a fully effective command headquarters again.

D Day was followed by ten days of intense and bitter fighting in which neither side was able to gain other than local, and often short-lived, advantage. There are times when the plans and aspirations of generals count for little. They must just sit back and watch as the soldiers of both sides slug it out, toe to toe, on the ground. To the private soldier, whose horizon probably extends no further than the next hedge which he must either capture or defend, the neatly-drawn Objectives and Phase Lines on the general's map would seem almost laughably irrelevent, if he knew of their existence. Battles are won and lost not, as history sometimes suggests, by generals, but by the those who must try to convert the general's plans into action. There is nothing clinical or exact in war; no battle goes according to plan. As Field Marshal Earl Wavell said in a wartime broadcast.

'War is a muddle; it is bound to be. There are so many incalculable accidents in the uncertain business – a turn in the weather which could not be foreseen; a message gone astray; a leader struck down at a critical moment. It is very rarely that even the best-laid plans go smoothly. The lesson is to realise this, and to provide, as far as possible, against the uncertainties of war – and not be surprised when they happen.'

That seems an admirable quotation for anyone who seeks to visit the Normandy battlefields and unearth the reality of what happened to those who fought there.

CHAPTER SIX

THE SUNKEN LANE, CRISTOT – 11 JUNE, D+5

The pressure which caused Panzer Lehr to call off its attack on Bayeux on 9 June centred around the capture of the small village of Audrieu by 1st Dorsets of 231 Brigade, and the advance further south by the tanks of 8 Armoured Brigade towards St Pierre and Tilly-sur-Seulles. A drive south through Audrieu, passing the Chateau, now an excellent hotel, leads onto the high ground of Le Haut d'Audrieu, Point 103, from where there are commanding views to the south and west. 4th/7th Royal Dragoon Guards secured this key area on 9 June. From here they watched a column of German tanks moving north-west through the low ground towards Bayeux – doubtless Major von Schönberg-Waldenberg leading his tank battalion of Panzer Lehr Division forward.

But while high ground, like Point 103, dominates the area, the fighting predominently took place in the close 'bocage' country. It was to be a slow and painful business for the British as they sought to expand their Normandy Beach-head. The Germans defended fiercely and the close country impeded the

The 'Bocage' was difficult country for the tanks of both sides. A German Panther forces its way forward.

movement and nullified the firepower of the advancing tanks. Much of the fighting occurred in confused, viscious, close-range encounters between the infantry of both sides. The advantage, in this country, always lay with the defender. The attacker must accept heavy casualties in gaining his objective. Nowhere was the fighting more fierce than in the fields astride a small sunken lane just south of the village of Cristot on 11 June, D+5.

After its D Day successes 6 Green Howards advance on D+1 was less dramatic. They secured the St Léger feature, including the main Caen-Bayeux road, and advanced a further two miles south until they overlooked the railway line just west of Le Bas

d'Audrieu, only to be pulled back to the St Leger feature later in the day, in line with the rest of 69 Infantry Brigade. On their right 151 Infantry Brigade established a position near the village of Condé-sur-Seulles. The Yorkshiremen were to remain there for the next three days.

'There was nothing more serious than a little sniping, some shelling and a determined and skilful recce by German armoured cars – just enough enemy activity to keep the soldiers from any real rest. Patrolling and a stand-to at 4.30 am and 11.30 pm made the nights unpleasantly short.'

LIEUTENANT COLONEL ROBIN HASTINGS

But Sunday 11 June was to prove to be a terrible day for 6 Green Howards. The rain was sheeting down. 'A lousy day for anything,' thought Company Sergeant Major Stan Hollis, 'anything, particularily war.' Hollis was still commanding 16 Platoon of D Company, and they were advancing again. A relatively simple operation, they had been told. They just had to capture a small hill, thereby protecting the left flank of 8 Armoured Brigade who were to advance south. The operation seemed to be something of a rush, and the experienced Hollis knew that hurried operations could sometimes lack the detailed planning and preparation needed to ensure success. It had been a quiet morning, with nothing unusual in the wind, but around

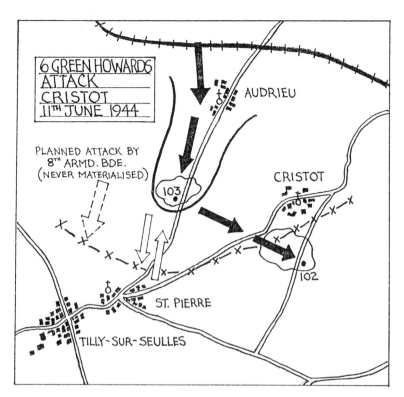

6 GREEN HOWARDS
ATTACK
CRISTOT
11TH JUNE 1944

AUDRIEU

PLANNED ATTACK BY
8TH ARMD. BDE.
(NEVER MATERIALISED)

103

CRISTOT

102

ST. PIERRE

TILLY-SUR-SEULLES

lunchtime Colonel Hastings had been summoned by the
commander of 69 Brigade. The Green Howards were to be ready
to move at 1400, for an unspecified task.

Hastings found his Brigadier, an elderly officer for whom he
had little respect, with Brigadier Cracroft of 8 Armoured
Brigade and Lieutenant Colonel Byron of 4/7 DG. 8 Armoured
Brigade, with 1 Dorsets and 8 Durham Light Infantry under
command, had earlier pushed forward south towards Tilly-sur-
Seulles. The Durhams had briefly secured entry into the village,
before being ejected by a German counter-attack. Another
attack was to be made. The two brigadiers had just returned
from a reconnaissance which had led them to a small hill just
south of the village of Cristot. Accompanied by B Squadron 4/7
DG they had managed to drive almost to the top of the hill,
encountering just a few Germans, who had been easily brushed
aside. If the hill was held by infantry, the flank of the armoured
advance would be protected. It would surely be a relatively
simple business to send an infantry battalion to occupy this key
piece of ground.

This, then, was the task for which Hastings and his

Yorkshiremen were required at such short notice. In concept it sounded simple, though as speed was clearly important and time short, Hastings was unable to carry out a reconnaissance. He was not enthusiastic, considering it to be something of a wild plunge into the unknown. But, as the earlier reconnaissance had not been seriously opposed, it seemed unlikely that the Germans would stay and dispute possession of the hill. He could only hope that the task would not prove too difficult.

Hastings'main worry was the country. This was the depth of the 'bocage'. The small fields and orchards were surrounded by thick, high hedges. A journey of some half a mile across country might involve crossing eight or more of these hedges. Furthermore, the country was interlaced with a network of narrow roads and tracks, often sunk deep between high banks, surmounted by hedges. With a view seldom further than about 80 yards, a few resolute men could easily hold up an advance of a large formation, causing many casualties. It was particularily unpleasant country for tanks which found the banks and hedges most difficult to cross. And, while they could not make best use of the long range of their tank guns, they were well within shot of any small infantry parties, which, armed with hand-held anti-tank weapons, might lie concealed in the hedges until a suitable target presented itself at almost unmissable range. Tank crews felt naked and vulnerable in this close country, and Hastings remembered the apprehension he had felt back in England when he first thought about fighting in the 'bocage'country.

He decided to advance with two companies leading; C on the left, B on the right. They would be accompanied by the tanks of B Squadron 4/7 DG. Behind them would follow D and A Companies with C Squadron, while A Squadron would bring forward the battalion's mortars and anti-tank guns once the objective had been captured. Between and just behind his two leading companies, Hastings'own headquarters would move up a convenient track which led towards the summit of the hill. This track would be the centre-line for the attack.

Initially the advance went without incident. But it was a nerve-racking business; each hedge proved to be something of a mental as well as a physical hurdle. As they forced their way through it the Yorkshiremen half expected their arrival in the next field to be greeted by a murderous hail of fire from some

British infantrymen slog it out yard by yard through the Normandy country lanes.

unseen Germans at very close range. Lack of preparatory time had prevented an artillery plan being arranged and registered. Fire support in the event of trouble would depend on the efficiency of the artillery obvervation officers, advancing with the leading companies.

Tucked away In the Normandy countrycide, Cristot is a difficult village to locate. Perhaps the simplest way to approach it is from Tilly-sur-Seulles. Take the **Caen road (D13) out of Tilly**, cross the River

Seulles, up a hill bending left and then right. As the road straightens out watch for a **narrow turning left marked Rue de Cristot**, just before a house. (If you pass large gates to a château you have gone too far!) Cristot is 3 kilometres along the D 172. About half way along there is a **T-junction**. **Turn right**. After a sharp left bend the road goes gently downhill. About three hundred yards after the bend, shortly before entering the village of Cristot, a narrow track, with high banks and trees on both sides, crosses the road. Pull in on the right and you will find yourself at the bottom of a sunken lane which marked the centre-line of the attack.

If, however, you are following the story on the ground, follow the D 82 south from the scene of Chapter 4 at Creully. After ½ mile **turn left** onto D 158B, signed Coulombs and Audrieu. Go through Coulombs, over the fly-over of the main Caen/Bayeux road, and through Loucelles. Just short of Audrieu there is a second fly-over, crossing the railway. The road enters Audrieu and joins the D 82, signed now to Tilly-sur-Seulles and Villers-Bocage. In the middle of **Audrieu**, opposite the church, **turn left**, signed Cristot. This small country road takes about six right-angle bends before it enters Cristot. At the **T junction** in Cristot **turn right**, and stop about 200 yards after leaving the village, where a narrow sunken lane crosses the road.

Walk up this lane on the east side (left if you are coming from Cristot village; right if coming from Tilly) until it rises to ground level. The trees astride the lane are much thinner than they were in 1944. To your left new farm buildings obscure a white house, which can be seen as you progress further up the lane. The French farmers have grubbed out many of the hedges, and the whole area looks much more open than it did all those years ago. In particular the field on your right was in fact about four separate fields, surrounded by high hedges. Looking half right you can see the top of the hill, more a gentle rise than a hill, about 400 yards ahead. This was the Green Howards objective. On 11 June 1944 it was hidden by the dense hedges and trees.

C and B Companies crossed the road south of Cristot without opposition and started to climb the gentle slope towards their objective. Suddenly C Company on the left came under withering fire from the area of the white farmhouse about 100 yards ahead. Almost immediately its commander, Captain Chambers, who had been wounded on the beach on D Day, was killed. He had only assumed command when Captain Linn was killed on D Day. It was, therefore, the second time in less than a week that C Company had seen their commander killed as he led them forward. As the infantry casualties mounted, so too some of the leading tanks of B Squadron were hit. On the left the attack ground to a halt.

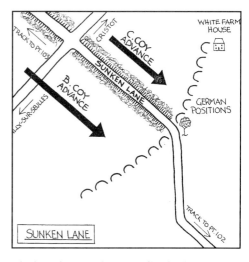

SUNKEN LANE

On the right B Company fared no better. It too came under heavy fire and the advance broke down, despite the efforts of Major Young, the company commander, who walked about the fields encouraging his men forward, in full view of the enemy, until he was wounded as he tried to outflank the German position. His life was saved by his runner, Private Leary, who, though wounded himself, managed to drag Young back into cover, dress his wounds and make certain that he was evacuated. (For his actions that day Leary was awarded the Military Medal.)

Hastings was now faced with something of a dilemma. Both his leading companies had been halted by heavy and totally unexpected fire, and had sustained many casualties, including both company commanders. In B Company the second-in-command, Captain Mitchell, had also been killed. But the battalion objective was still some way ahead, and was clearly far more strongly defended than had been anticipated. Hastings decided upon another tack. A Company, moving behind B Company on the right, would take over the lead and try to outflank the enemy, thereby continuing the advance as well as taking some of the pressure off the battered B and C Companies. Having given orders for this, Hastings set about trying to sort out the confusion in these two companies. But as he and his small headquarters moved up the narrow track they too came under fire. A battalion headquarters is neither strong enough nor properly equipped to deal with a strongly held enemy position. Hastings withdrew quickly to the road and called up his sole remaining reserve, D Company. When Major Lofthouse joined him at the road/track junction, Hastings ordered him to clear the track ahead.

Lofthouse made a quick and simple plan. D Company would advance up the track with 16 Platoon on the left and 17 and 18

Platoons on the right. Hollis, at the head of 16 Platoon, was to keep level with 17 Platoon, with a tank moving slowly up the track between the two platoons.

D Company moved gingerly forward. They could hear the heavy firing in the fields on both sides of them; at least the high banks of the lane would give them some protection. But, conversely, they would be completely exposed to fire coming down the track. They had advanced about two-thirds of the way when they were greeted by a short burst of fire. Hollis knew that sound immediately – the tell-tale rapid burst of a Spandau machine-gun. On his right the tank had stopped, and he could see that 17 Platoon had already taken casualties. Clearly the machine-gun was sited at the far end of the lane, dominating the entire approach. Hollis crawled forward a little to see whether he could pin-point the source of the trouble. Suddenly his eye was caught by a slight movement at the foot of a tree at the end of the lane. The exact spot is arrowed on the photograph opposite. Hollis was half way up the lane on the left. As he

German Spandau team operating in the lanes of the bocage. CSM Hollis took two machine gunners on in a frontal attack in the sunken lane.

German machine gunners at the head of the lane (arrowed) were holding up the Green Howards – CSM Hollis, noted their methodical operation of the weapon and timed his attack accordingly.

watched, two heads appeared above a mound of earth. Their appearance was followed by a sharp burst of fire which hammered down the track. The heads then quickly bobbed down behind their cover. Hollis continued to watch. After a few seconds the heads appeared again, fired another burst and

CSM Stan Hollis VC

again disappeared. And again... and again. Hollis noticed how methodical they were. 'Typically German – carefully observing a reguation burst and a regulation pause.' To Hollis this was intolerable. Why should two stereotyped Germans be allowed to hold up the advance and cause these casualties? The situation demanded instant action. Their next burst, he vowed, would be their last.

Opening his ammunition pouch Hollis fumbled around inside for a grenade. But all his hand drew out was a shaving brush and a pair of socks. Cursing his lack of preparedness he turned to one of his soldiers and demanded a grenade. This was quickly produced. As the Germans ducked down after the next burst he flung the grenade. As his fingers released it he realised with horror that he had forgotten to pull out the safety pin. But where most men would have started again with another grenade, Hollis could not wait that long. In the split second that it took for the grenade to land just short of the mound, he realised that although he knew that the grenade would not explode, the Germans did not. It was only human nature that they would wait crouching behind their cover until the grenade had exploded. So they crouched and waited. This was the position in which Hollis found them a few seconds later, after a quick solo dash up the lane. One burst from his Sten gun and the way was clear for D Company to continue the advance.

Following on behind, Hastings reached the point where the sunken lane rises to ground level. He paused to take stock by the tree where Hollis just despatched the two Germans. To his right he could see that A and B Companies had joined up and were nearing the far end of the field. To his left, too, things looked a little better. C Company had just managed to capture the white farmhouse. Several tanks were burning in the field. One, clearly out of control, was driving round and round in a tight circle like some macabre merry-go-round. The fields on both sides seemed full of casualties and a consider-able number of German prisoners were being herded together. But two points were abundantly clear. First, any idea of a quick and easy move to occupy some almost undefended hill was clearly wrong. The place was alive with Germans, who were clearly of a quality not hitherto encountered by the Green

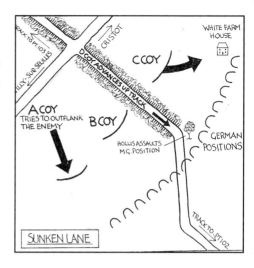

Howards since they had come ashore five days before. Secondly, casualties in the close fighting against this most resolute enemy, who had almost physically to be dug out of his positions, were extremely high and still mounting, and the final objective was still several hundred yards ahead. Hastings took a deep breath, and ordered the attack to push on.

Doggedly the Yorkshiremen fought their way forward against an enemy equally determined not to give ground. A little further on, Major Honeyman, A Company Commander, reported that his sergeant-major had gone forward to try to extricate part of a platoon which had advanced a little too far, and was himself pinned down by German machine-gun fire. Honeyman asked his Colonel's permission to go forward to help him. Hastings was not enthusiastic. Honeyman could go forward a bit to see if he could locate the exact position and possibly signal to them, but he was not to get involved in any foolhardy attempt to get them out. Honeyman made his way slowly forward, but had gone only a short distance when, peering over a hedge to see if he could locate his men, he was shot in the head and killed. This was tragedy indeed. Honeyman had already proved to be an outstanding company commander. He died before the announcement that he had been awarded the Military Cross for his leadership of A Company on King Beach on D Day. Ironically Company Sergeant Major Calvert brought his party back safely about an hour later, having fought an extremely gallant and determined action, for which he was later awarded the Distinguished Conduct Medal.

Clearly the attack had again stuck fast, and, with the tanks also unable to move forward, Hastings had no alternative but to order his battalion to halt. Once again he considered the situation. A and B Companies now only had one officer left each; C and D had two each. A large number of key NCOs were also dead or wounded. Hastings ordered the battalion to prepare to hold the ground they had taken. They had shot their bolt; if Brigade Headquarters still wanted the summit of the hill, then another battalion would have to pass through 6 Green Howards in order to take it.

For some hours the battalion held their position. Among those who worked tirelessly that dreadful evening was Padre Henry Lovegrove. A much respected member of the battalion, Lovegrove seemed oblivious to the constant fire as he tended the wounded and looked after the dead and the dying. He was to be awarded the Military Cross for his actions that day. As the evening wore on Hastings heard the sound of heavy fighting behind him, across the other side of the road in the area of Point 103, from which the Yorkshiremen had launched their attack. Clearly a German counter-attack was in danger of cutting them off. It was now beginning to get dark, and the feeling of growing isolation was compounded by knowledge of the fact that the tanks of the 4/7 DG would shortly have to pull back to a safe area to carry out their normal night-time maintenance. Hastings radioed back to his brigadier, and was somewhat relieved when his advice that his battalion should withdraw was accepted. This was achieved with the tanks of the 4/7 DG carrying back as many of the Green Howards wounded as could be recovered.

11 June was as bad a day for 6 Green Howards as could possible be imagined. They had suffered nearly 250 casualties in just a few hours fighting. In short, the nucleus of a fine battalion had been lost, with nothing to show for it.

'There were innumerable lessons to be learned from this attack. It occurred at a time when the Army's initial advance was losing impetus; the contact battle was merging into static warfare. Those are difficult and often expensive moments. Certainly the enemy were not deeply entrenched, but were using the natural cover and protection of hedgerow and ditch. In this thick leafy country the advantage is with the defenders, who can stay still and hold their fire until the last moment. Tanks are blind in this country. By 11 June the enemy was recovering from his first shock. He was fighting to the death. It was too late to

plunge into deep unrecced country with insufficient knowledge of the strength or disposition of the enemy.'

LIEUTENANT-COLONEL ROBIN HASTINGS

The attack on Tilly-sur-Seulles by 8 Armoured Brigade never materialised. The Germans struck first, with the tanks of 2nd Battalion Panzer Lehr Regiment advancing north towards Point 103, the high ground at Le Haut d'Audrieu. Four German tanks managed to break into the British position there before they were destroyed and the rest driven off. In this brief but fierce battle Major von Schönberg-Waldenberg, as ever at the head of his battalion, was killed. The rest then withdrew back to the Tilly area, licking their wounds. It was the sound of this fighting which Hastings heard behind him, as he and his Yorkshiremen struggled to secure the ground that they had won at such cost.

The battle for the Sunken Lane was just one of many small, local but fierce encounters as the Allies systematically ground-down the German forces in the weeks following D Day. It was one of those remarkable coincidences of war that both sides should seek to secure that small Hill 102 near Cristot at almost the same time. To the British it was just a matter of flank

Colonel Hastings at the Sunken Lane in 1975.

British troops moving up through the hedgerows – a nerve-racking experience.

Cristot church. The scene shortly after the fight in the sunken lane.

Cristot church today.

protection for an impending attack. To the Germans it was vital ground in their defence of the area. As can be seen from the top, the view to the east and south is one of long fields of view and fire, very different from the close bocage country to the west. Indeed the view stretches almost to Carpiquet airfield and the outskirts of Caen. Had the Green Howards taken this hill on D+5, as they so nearly did, the entire German position west of Caen would have become most unpleasant. Look at the ring contours on a map and none of this is apparent. It is not surprising that none of the British commanders realised the true significance of that hill until, on 25 Jun, D+19, it was finally taken. Only then did it become clear why soldiers from 12 SS Panzer Division (*Hitlerjugend*) were so quickly moved there, by chance between the two brigadiers' reconnaissance and the Green Howards attack.

So often there exists an unwritten chivalry in war. Like the boxer who strives to knock out his opponent, but would never continue the assault as his victim lies unconscious on the floor, so in war, the treatment of enemy casualties and prisoners is almost invariably sympathetic and correct. The medical services of both sides treat enemy casualties with the same care that they treat their own. There are frequent stories of the gallantry of medical staff, collecting casualties, both friend and foe, under intense fire. It seems that to both sides, even in the heat of battle, the sight of the medical officer, with the Red Cross on his

Treatment of enemy casualties and prisoners is almost invariably sympathetic. This young soldier of the Wehrmacht, in obvious distress, receives attention from an American soldier. Had he been a member of an SS unit his chances for survival after surrendering would have been considerably less.

vehicle, is respected; he is probably not fired upon intentionally. But this chivalry does not seem to have extended to the 12 SS Panzer Division (*Hitlerjugend*). Those who fought against the Hitler Youth in Normandy show none of the respect with which they now talk about most of their former enemies. A bitterness tends to creep into their voices, ever after more than 50 years. The story of the 'execution'of 50 Canadian prisoners at Audrieu on 8 June is well chronicled and has coloured the view of many.

The battle for the Sunken Lane has its own nasty epilogue. Among those wounded and captured was a young Lieutenant of the 4/7 DG. Shortly after the battle two men from the regiment visited his mother in England to say that he had been seen to be wounded and was probably now a prisoner of war. 'No', she replied, 'he's dead.' When the two suggested that there was no proof of this she said that his labrador, which normally lay quietly in the corner of the room suddenly started to whine at about 6pm on 11 June. It whined until 9pm, then curled up and went quietly to sleep. 'I know', said the mother, 'that that was when he was dying'. Only later in the war did the horrific truth emerge. A soldier of 12 SS was captured by the British during the Falaise battle in August. Under interrogation he told the story of a wounded British officer who was captured and tied to the broken limb of a tree. Whenever the British artillery opened up on the German position he was dragged out into the open. He took 3 hours to die. Research pinpointed this story to Hill 102 near Cristot, from 6 to 9pm on 11 June. War is indeed a gruesome business.

To follow these battles conveniently on the ground, rather than in the strictly chronological order in which they are laid out in this book, go next to Lingèvres, Chapter 8. From the Sunken Lane, follow the D 172 south-west to Tilly-sur-Seulles. On joining the D 13 on the edge of Tilly, **turn right**, go through the town and on west. Shortly after leaving Tilly you will pass the Commonwealth War Graves Cemetery, where lie buried many of those who died in the intensive fighting in the area in June 1944. Continue west for 1½ miles until you reach Lingèvres.

CHAPTER SEVEN

DISASTER AT VILLERS-BOCAGE – 13 JUNE, D+7

It was 12 June, D+6, and Lieutenant Colonel Desmond Gordon was delighted. He had just been told that 1st/7th Battalion The Queen's Regiment, a Lorried Infantry Battalion which he commanded in 131 Infantry Brigade of 7 Armoured Division, was to move forward as quickly as possible to join 22 Armoured Brigade. Delighted on two accounts. First, the armoured brigade was to lead a deep thrust into the German lines, and he was keen that his Queensmen should be at the front of it. Secondly, while he did not greatly respect his Infantry Brigade Commander, the prospect of coming under command of Brigadier Robert 'Looney' Hinde was immensely encouraging.

Armoured divisions consisted, in Normandy in June 1944, of one armoured brigade of three regiments of tanks and a motor battalion of infantry in half-track vehicles, and one lorried infantry brigade of three infantry battalions. The weakness of this organisation was that the motor battalion, formed in most armoured divisions by battalions of the 60th Rifles and The Rifle

Colonel Gordon escorts General Montgomery on a visit to 1/7 Queens shortly before D-Day.

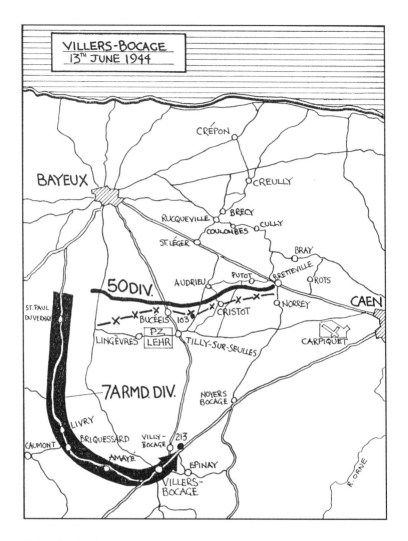

Brigade, had so many men tied up in the specialist tasks of drivers, gunners and radio operators, that a platoon, dismounting on its feet, was woefully short of Riflemen to clear an enemy position. Furthermore, 1st Battalion The Rifle Brigade, the motor battalion in 22 Armoured Brigade was still short of one company which had not yet arrived from England. Aware of a need for more Infantry for this operation, Brigadier Hinde had asked the divisional commander, Major General Bobby Erskine, for another infantry battalion. Lieutenant Colonel Gordon's 1/7 Queens would join 22 Armoured Brigade, while

Lieutenant Colonel Carver's 1 Royal Tank Regiment made the reverse journey.

As light faded 1/7 Queens started its move forward, and within minutes all were covered with a film of dusk and grime thrown up by the lorries as they moved up. By dawn next morning they had caught up with the rest of 22 Brigade near Livry – a welcome chance to clean up men and weapons, have that essential requirement for any soldier, a 'brew' of tea, allow the stragglers to catch up, and, for Gordon, to find out what was in store for them.

Two days earlier, on 10 June, 7 Armoured Division had passed through 50 Division astride the Bayeux – Tilly-sur-Seulles road, and pressed on south. By dusk the leading elements had reached Bucéels, just two miles north of Tilly. But here they ran head-on into Panzer Lehr Division which had been ordered to advance on Bayeux. Little progress was made next day. Early on 12 June Generals Bucknall of 30 Corps and Erskine of 7 Armoured Division discussed the future. Intelligence suggested that there might be a gap in the German defences between Caumont, now under attack by the Americans, and Panzer Lehr in the Tilly-sur-Seulles area. If 7 Armoured Division could launch a swift right hook, through St Paul-du-Vernay, Livry, Briquessard, Amayé and on to Villers-Bocage and the high ground north-east of it, it might cut-off Panzer Lehr in the Tilly and Lingèvres areas.

22 Armoured Brigade led the thrust which went well until held up around 1600 in the Livry area. By 2000 the opposition had been cleared by a motor company of 1 RB, but it was decided to halt the advance for the night, in order to allow the rest of the division to catch up, essential maintenance to take place, and contact to be made with the Americans who were attacking Caumont on the right. Doubtless the decision to halt made sense at the time, but, in the light of the events that followed next day it was a pity that Brigadier Hinde did not push on the remaining six miles, securing Villers-Bocage that night. But war is full of 'if onlys'!

Very early on 13 June Hinde gave orders to his commanding officers. Surprisingly he decided not to lead with his reconnaissance regiment, 8th King's Royal Irish Hussars, as would have been normal when advancing out of contact with the enemy. The tanks of 4 County of London Yeomanry

(Sharpshooters), with A Company 1 RB under command, would lead through Villers-Bocage and on to the high ground of Point 213 about a mile north-east of the town on the Caen road. 1/7 Queens would secure the town east of the church, while the rest of 1 RB held the western end. 5 RTR would take the high ground near Maisoncelles-Pelvey, 2 miles south-west of Villers-Bocage and the 17-pounder self-propelled guns of 260 Anti-tank Battery, Royal Artillery would provide a screen between the two tank regiments, covering the approaches from the south-east.

22 Armoured Brigade moved forward at 0530 on 13 June. A Squadron of the Sharpshooters, with the half-tracks of A Company and two 6-pounder anti-tank guns of 1 RB tucked in behind, passed through Amayé and reached Villers-Bocage at about 0800. Stopping to ask some French civilians whether there were any Germans in the town, they were delighted to hear that it was clear. Lieutenant Colonel Lord Cranley, the Sharpshooters commanding officer, keen to secure his objective as quickly as possible, ordered Major Scott's A Squadron to press on to the high ground beyond the town. The rest of the regiment would halt in the town until they heard that that Point 213 had been captured. This would also give the crews a welcome chance to check over the tanks and grab a quick bite of breakfast, neither of which had been possible in the rush to press on quickly that morning. The A Squadron/A Company group motored on through the town, bending left at the end of the main street and climbing the hill beyond.

Cromwells belonging to the 7th Armoured Division advancing through the Bocage.

To ensure that the objective was firmly in his hands, Cranley decided to follow the leading squadron closely himself. He could then call forward the rest of the regiment, leaving the infantry of 1/7 Queens and 1 RB to secure the town itself. He moved off with the four Cromwell tanks that constituted his Regimental Headquarters – his own tank, that of his second-in-command Major Carr, the Regimental-Sergeant Major's tank, and Captain Dyas in a spare tank, with a Daimler scout car also in tow. Shortly after passing the bend at the top of the main street he halted this group, left the tanks behind and went forward in his scout car to join A Squadron, who had reached Point 213 unmolested. All seemed to be going entirely according to plan. Doubtless Panzer Lehr Division was full committed facing 50 Division further north, unaware of the threat mounting behind them.

To reach the battlefield of Villers-Bocage, take the D6 south from Tilly-sur-Seulles. About one mile south of Tilly the road crosses the D9, which involves **turning left** along the D9 for about 200 yards, over the River Seulles and **immediately right**, signed for Villers-Bocage. Follow the D6 for about five miles to a **junction** at the east end of the town. **Turn hard left**, and you will see a straight road climbing the hill ahead of you. It is the summit of that hill which is your destination, though the route to it is less simple than it looks. Follow the road under the new N175 dual carriageway bridge, then keep left until you rejoin the old N175 to Caen. Shortly after rejoining it, look right down a small road which runs through Montbrocq to Epinay – this plays an important part in the story. Then proceed to the summit. This is Point 213, reached by A squadron of the Sharpshooters at about 0815 on the morning of 13 June 1944. Once there you will realise why this was such an important objective. The view of the road ahead stretches for miles. Locate a small turning to the left, just by a cottage, with a gate in the fence opposite – call it Milner's Gate, which will mean something later in the story. Because of the new dual carriageway, this small road ends abruptly in a bank, after just a couple of hundred yards. Turn round and park on the main road where you can look down the hill, towards Villers-Bocage.

The first part of the story of the battle takes place near the Montbrocq turning, down the hill in front of you. It then moves to the middle of the town. But the action returns to Point 213 later in the morning, so it is worth taking a mental picture of the scene before leaving for the town centre. Picture, if you can in today's tranquil scene, a squadron of tanks just arriving at Point 213. Behind, climbing the hill from Villers-Bocage are the carriers and half-tracks of the motor infantry company.

Lieutenant Michael Wittmann was already a legend in the German Army. His tally of armoured vehicles knocked-out stood at 119 and he held the Iron Cross 1st and 2nd Class and the Knight's Cross, to which had already been added the Oak Leaves. For his actions this day he would later add the Swords to his Knight's Cross, and be promoted Captain. But as dawn broke on the morning 13 June he had no idea, as commander of 2 Company of 101 SS Heavy Tank Battalion, that action was imminent. On D Day, just a week before, 101 SS had been at Beauvais, near Paris. Given hasty orders to move to Normandy, they had arrived in the Villers-Bocage area on the afternoon of 12 June. 2 Company now consisted of just five Tiger tanks, having suffered from the close attention of the Allied Air Forces during their move to Normandy. They spent the night 12/13 June in a small wood just south of the small hamlet of Montbrocq, about a mile north-east of the town. Rumours are

Wittmann's gun aimer Balthasar Woll (above) and Michael Wittmann – an effective tank killer team. The German ace accounted for 138 enemy tanks destroyed.

Wittman's Tigers, SS Panzer Abteilung 101, three days before the action at Villers-Bocage.

frequent in war, and the rumour that night was that a British armoured force was trying to outflank and cut off Panzer Lehr Division. So, early on 13 June Wittmann decided to investigate the truth of this rumour. Leaving his other tanks to carry out their normal morning maintenance (much needed after an arduous journey), Wittmann opted to explore on his own. He would go through Villers Bocage and head north-west towards Balleroy to see whether he could locate any British advance. He did not have far to look.

Shortly after moving off he met an aggitated German sergeant in the woods just south of the Villers-Bocage/Caen road. There were the ominous noises of tanks grinding up the hill from the town, and yet there were no German tanks in the area. Leaving his Tiger tank behind, Wittmann crawled forward and peered through a hedge, to see A Squadron of the Sharpshooters heading up the slope towards Point 213. The Cromwell tanks and the accompanying infantry half-tracks would be easy meat for a Tiger's 88mm gun; nor would the 75mm gun on the Cromwells pose much of a threat to the heavily-armoured German.

It must have been shortly after 0830 that Wittmann's vast Tiger tank 'expoded' into the midst of the British force. The leading elements of A Squadron, having reached their objective

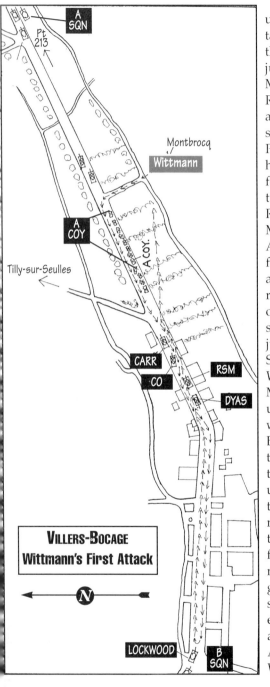

A
SQN

Pt
213

Montbrocq

Wittmann

A
COY

A COY.

Tilly-sur-Seulles

CARR

CO

RSM

DYAS

VILLERS-BOCAGE
Wittmann's First Attack

N

LOCKWOOD

B
SQN

unopposed, were confidently taking-stock of their position. At the front Colonel Cranley had just joined Major Scott and Major Wright of A Company 1 RB. Many of the tank crews already had a 'brew' on. Behind, still climbing the slope towards Point 213, were the carriers and half-tracks of A Company followed by the light 'Honey' tanks of the Sharpshooter's Reconnaissance Troop. Captain Milner, second-in-command of A Company, was bringing forward some junior officers and a section of Riflemen, in order to receive orders for the next phase of the operation from their seniors at the front. They had just passed the last two Sharpshooters tanks, when Wittmann struck, from the Montbrocq track, about half way up the hill. Milner could only watch helplessly as the two British tanks frantically tried to traverse and depress their guns to engage the Tiger advancing up the slope towards them. At times like this, when instant reaction is called for, the power traverse of a turret must seem frustratingly slow. They never made it. Wittmann's huge 88mm gun erupted, and the first two shots destroyed both tanks, effectively blocking the road, and thereby isolating the rest of A Squadron up at Point 213. Wittmann now turned his attention towards the town and the rear of the British column. Within minutes most of the half-tracks of A Company 1RB, which were strung out along the road from Villers-Bocage, were ablaze as Wittmann motored down the line. One 6-pounder anti-tank gun, manned by Sergeant Bray and his crew of Riflemen, swung quickly into action – and was blown to bits by the mighty Tiger's gun. The road was strewn with bodies and burning vehicles, while men sought what cover they could find in the ditches and hedges. Further up the slope towards Point 213, Milner could only watch this carnage with horror.

Satisfied that he had blocked any chance of a British withdrawal, Wittmann left this scene of mayhem behind him and motored on down into Villers-Bocage in search of further easy pickings. Next he met the light Honey tanks of the Sharpshooters Reconnaissance Troop. They, too, proved to be no match for the Tiger; within a few seconds all were reduced to burning hulks.

Now is the time to follow Wittmann's route down into Villers-Bocage, taking with you a clear picture of Point 213. **Drive back down the hill**, under the dual carriage-way and on into the town. Shortly before the road bends right, from near the garage on the right, you will be able to compare the view with the picture on page 118. Park near the TOTAL Garage and turn to face the road towards Point 213 (photo p110). The tanks of RHQ were parked in the area of the pedestrian crossings ahead of you.

A Sherman Firefly on the hill to Point 213. The gun traversed to meet the threat from Wittmann's Tiger – but never made it.

Carnage on the road leading up to Point 213. The remains of the anti-tank guns of A Coy IRB after Wittmann's struck.

British dead littered the roadside ditch at Point 213.

In Villers-Bocage main street, Major Carr saw the smoke and heard the noise of firing ahead at Pt 213. A Squadron had either encountered an enemy force or come under artillery fire. Perhaps the Colonel, who was up with A Squadron, would need further reinforcements. Leaving the other RHQ tanks, Carr decided to investigate. He started to drive towards Point 213 – and met a Tiger tank advancing towards him out of the smoke. Following a quick order to his gunner to fire, he watched in dismay as the 75mm shell bounced off the Tiger's armour, without even slowing the German's progress. Wittmann's gunner replied, and within seconds Carr's tank was a blazing inferno, with all the crew dead or wounded. Wittmann drove calmly past the wreck and, with his next shot, similarily destroyed the

Easy pickings – a knocked-out Honey of the Sharpshooters Reconnaissance Troop.

Colonel's tank. The RSM had already started a hasty withdrawal. He had not got far before a third shell from the Tiger crashed into his tank. With every prospect of more successes ahead Wittmann pressed on, round the bend and down the main street towards the road junction at the far end.

The remaining Cromwell tank in the RHQ group was that of Captain Pat Dyas. Wounded in the North African desert in 1942, Dyas had only rejoined the Sharp-shooters shortly before D Day,

Captain Pat Dyas

although no specific appointment was avail-able. He would come 'as spare captain in RHQ; we'll doubtless find something for you'. And so, with that rather imprecise role, Dyas was commanding the fourth RHQ tank in Villers-Bocage that morning. Prudently, when the other three tanks stopped in the main street, Dyas had backed his tank into a garden at right-angles to the street – and waited.

There are some days when every fall of the dice seems to bring mis-fortune. It was misfortune that Colonel Cranley and A Squadron group were now isolated at Point 213.

Looking northeast from Villers-Bocage towards the high ground of Pt 213, 1998. When Wittmann struck, A Squadron was at the top of the hill, A Company strung out on the slope towards it. Wittmann motored down this road into the town and destroyed the tanks of RHQ in the area where the cars are shown on this photograph.

It was misfortune that Major Carr, the regimental second-in-command was now a casualty. And it was misfortune indeed that shortly before Wittmann made his dramatic entry into Villers-Bocage that morning, Dyas' gunner had asked permission to leave the tank 'to answer the call of nature'. Dyas agreed, but, having heard the sound of gunfire ahead, told him to run over to the Colonel's tank and try to find out what was going on. Had Wittmann passed the muzzle of Dyas' gun five minutes earlier or later, an armoured-piercing round, at a range less than 20 yards, would doubtless have ended his journey there and then – a broken track or a jammed turret would have sufficed. Although the Cromwell's 75mm gun could not penetrate the Tiger's frontal or side armour, it could certainly have blown off a track at point-blank range. Dyas heard the Colonel's and RSM's tanks explode. Quickly he ordered his wireless operator to climb into the gunner's seat and prepare for action. But it was too late. To his utter frustration, Dyas could only watch Wittmann's huge Tiger tank lumber by, its commander oblivious of the threat to his flank. Perhaps fortune favours the brave, in which case Wittmann was admirably qualified for his ample supply of luck.

As soon as his new gunner was installed, Dyas ordered the driver to start up and 'follow that tank'. If he could sneak up on the Tiger from behind he might be able to destroy it with a shot in its more thinly armoured rear. The Cromwell swung out left onto the main street as Dyas set about stalking his prey.

On reaching the Caumont junction at the west end of the main street Wittmann ordered the driver to slow down. Peering round the corner to the right he could make out the long barrel of a Sherman Firefly's 17-pounder gun. Simultaneously, Sergeant Lockwood, the Firefly

Liutenant-Colonel Lord Cranley, Commanding Officer of the Sharpshooters.

commander, hearing the clatter of tank tracks and, expecting it to be one of his own regimental tanks returning from further forward, realised with horror that he was confronted by the vast outline of a Tiger tank. Frantically he ordered 'Tank Action'. Wittmann fired first and the shop behind Lockwood's tank collapsed in a shower of rubble and dust. Lockwood returned fire, but his shot merely glanced off the angled plates of the Tiger's turret.

Realising that he was now confronting a sizeable force, Wittmann quickly reversed out of trouble, turned his tank round and drove back up the main street again, round the bend

Looking west along the main street. Wittmann's Tiger met Lockwood's Firefly at the junction at the far end.

at the top – and met Dyas' Cromwell. As it advanced towards him Dyas realised that it was not the vulnerable rear of the Tiger that now confronted him, but its thickly armoured front. But the Tiger's formidable gun was pointing the other way, towards the obvious threat from which it had just retired. This gave Dyas sufficient time to get off two rounds, as he watched the German turret traverse slowly round towards him. Both rounds struck the Tiger squarely at a range of about 70 yards – and, to Dyas' utter dismay, both rounds bounced-off. Neither halted nor even slowed the advancing German. By now the Tiger's gun had swung round onto the Cromwell, and, as Dyas and his crew tried frantically to fire again, one round of 88mm crashed into their tank, hitting it at the bottom of the turret. The effect was devastating. Dyas was blown clean out of the tank, landing on the road. The acting-gunner was killed instantly. And the driver, who managed to clamber out of the stricken tank, was cut down by a burst of machine-gun fire as he ran across the road. Within a few minutes a column of smoke was spiralling up from the tank. Wittmann continued his journey east, passing the wrecks of the four Sharpshooters RHQ tanks, his own undamaged by at least five British hits.

Dyas could only watch him go, before crossing the road to the

Captain Dyas' Cromwell tank after its encounter with Wittmann's Tiger. To the right is the road towards Pt 213.

RSM's tank. Here he found the wireless headset hanging outside the tank. He was quickly able to contact Colonel Cranley, still forward with A Squadron at Point 213, tell him of the devastation in the town, and warn him that a Tiger tank was moving east towards him. Cranley replied that they, too, were under attack. As Dyas spoke to his commanding officer, a burst of machine-gun fire from the withdrawing German whipped over his head, causing him to cut short the conversation and dive over a nearby hedge into a small garden. To his amazement he found a young French girl hiding in the garden. Together they hid briefly in a pigsty while she explained, remarkably calmly considering the machine-gun rounds passing just overhead, that she knew all the back alleys of Villers-Bocage. She then proceeded to lead Dyas safely back to join the rest of the Sharpshooters at the west end of the town. On arrival he explained to Major Aird, B Squadron commander, that the Colonel and A Squadron were cut off and that Major Carr, the second-in-command, was either dead or seriously wounded. Without further delay Major Aird assumed command of the Sharpshooters and told Dyas to take over as Adjutant.

Among those at Point 213 Captain Christopher Milner, second-in-command of A Company 1 RB, had not been idle. Having watched Wittmann's first strike, he had immediately set about sorting out the chaos. With the company commander, Major Wright, up ahead with Colonel Cranley, he effectively took over command of the remainder of A Company. He posted sentries to ensure that they were not caught napping again, organised a hasty defensive position, and arranged for the treatment of the wounded. While he was frantically busy, up at Point 213 there was something of a lull, as the Colonel tried to find out what was happening and decide what to do. Vehicle movement back from the high ground was effectively cut off by the burning tanks blocking the road. It is difficult to be exact about the sequence and timings of events at Point 213. When Cranley told Dyas that they were under attack, it seems most likely that he was actually reflecting Wittmann's first strike, largely on A Company 1 RB. While action may begin suddenly, in a surprise strike, it seldom ends quickly. With two of A Squadron's tanks, the carriers and half-tracks of A Company and the Honey tanks of the Reconnaissance Troop all destroyed, and countless dead and wounded, the confusion of battle will certainly have lasted some time. It is entirely reasonable that the commanding officer, on the top of Point 213, a quarter of a mile from the attack, might think, when he spoke to Dyas probably about 15 to 20 minutes later, that they were still under attack, although, with the advantage if hindsight, this seems unlikely.

It was, perhaps, an hour and a half later that Milner heard the noise of tanks approaching. Doubtless this was a relief force on its way to reinforce them. That hope was short-lived, when the other four Tiger tanks of Wittmann's company struck, doubtless responding to radio orders from their commander. Systematically they destroyed all the remaining A Squadron tanks and machine-gunned anyone who moved. The Cromwells and Shermans proved no match for the vastly more powerful Tigers. Within a few minutes all were reduced to burning wrecks. A Squadron of the Sharpshooters had virtually ceased to exist. The battle, if battle it could be called, was brief, brutal and totally one-sided. The crews could only take what cover they could find from the withering fire. As the German tanks

A Cromwell – no match for the Tigers and Panthers – blazes away after receiving a direct hit.

Point 213 German troops examine the destroyed tanks of A Squadron of the Sharpshooters.

moved on, German infantry started to round-up those who had survived. Among the dead was A Squadron commander, Major Scott. Colonel Cranley, Major Wright, A Company commander, and all those still alive at Point 213 became prisoners-of-war – all except Milner.

As the German infantry started to round up the survivors, Milner was near the summit, where a small lane runs off north from the main road, beside a cottage. Capture or escape were the only options, and Milner just had time to run through the gate into the orchard on the right of the lane, hoping that he had not been seen. But an alert German infantryman had noticed his flight and proceeded to stalk him, calling on him to surrender. To avoid capture and get a better view of the German locations, Milner climbed a tree in the orchard – and found an enemy unit setting up a defensive position just a few yards away, on the far side of a hedge below his tree. Clearly escape was not going to be easy; it might be sensible to await nightfall. When, as he watched and waited, a British artillery bombardment fell on the area, he decided that he would use this to cover his escape. Descending quickly from his tree, he crawled out of the orchard,

Point 213 in 1998. The gate on the left by the cul-de-sac sign is where Captain Milner escaped.

Captain Milner escaped through this gate

found a convenient and well-concealed dip in the ground, curled up and slept till dusk.

After dark, Milner set out to rejoin the rest of 1 RB west of Villers-Bocage. He crossed the road and took a wide flanking course south. It proved to be an eventful journey. Early on he found a farm trough in a field. Realising that he had had nothing to eat or drink that day, he filled his beret and had a satisfying drink before moving on. At one stage, alerted by the sound of heavy snores, he found himself in the middle of a German infantry position. Fortunately they had failed to post a sentry – all were sleeping, with their rifles piled up in the centre. Mastering the urge to waken them rudely with a burst of fire or a grenade, he crept on. Some time later he was challenged by a British voice, but, aware that itchy fingers would be on triggers that night, he thought it prudent to melt back into the dark. A Verey pistol fired, and he just had time to dive over a nearby bank before the illuminating flare burst overhead. After a pause to allow things to quieten down he continued his hazardous journey. It was with some relief that, around dawn on 14 June, Milner met 5 RTR, south-west of Villers-Bocage – the only man to escape from the mayhem at Point 213.

Another who was lucky not to be caught in the action on the road to Point 213 was Brigadier Hinde. He had followed Colonel Cranley forward and must have witnessed some of Wittmann's slaughter of A Company and the Reconnaissance Troop, before rapidly retracing his steps back through the town. At about 1000 he ordered 1/7 Queens to move into Villers-Bocage. Thereafter he seems to have disappeared from the battlefield, not reappearing until late in the afternoon. Colonel Gordon, the Queens commanding officer, quickly sent forward his Anti-tank Platoon, while the rifle companies dismounted from their lorries at Amayé and walked the two miles into Villers-Bocage, arriving sometime after 1100.

On leaving the town Wittmann had returned to his company, changed to a different tank and, accompanied by two of his Tigers which had just destroyed A Squadron at Point 213, and one Mk4 tank, he returned once again to the town centre of Villers-Bocage. But by now the British were waiting. Major Aird, now commanding the Sharpshooters, had despatched Lieutenant Cotton and his troop to move round the southern outskirts of the town, avoiding the main street, and try to reach Point 213. After a short brush with some Germans on the edge of the town, Cotton considered it unwise to try to cross the difficult railway embankment and swan off into open country with his troop. Prudently he returned to the town centre and established a well-prepared ambush position. With his tanks concealed and set back from the main street, in the area of the town square, he hoped to get a short-range flanking shoot at any enemy tank driving along the main street. Determined not to miss, Cotton ensured that his tank guns were sited through the gun barrels at easily identifiable marks on the opposite walls. He and his troop waited. And in a narrow alley just further west Colonel Gordon of 1/7 Queens similarily deployed a 6-pounder anti-tank gun. Wittmann's luck was about to run out; the trap was baited, and it was a trap into which he and his tanks were about to enter.

Once again Wittmann drove down the main street of Villers-Bocage, passing the now smouldering remains of the four RHQ tanks which he had earlier destroyed. The action that followed was short, sharp and conclusive. Wittmann

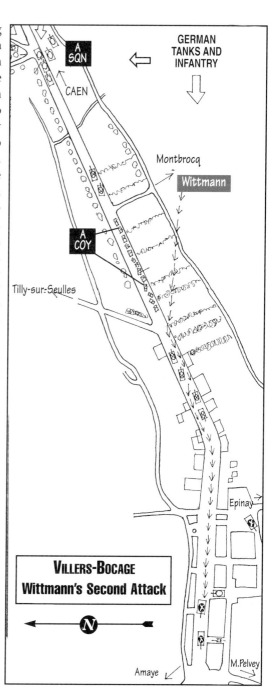

GERMAN TANKS AND INFANTRY

CAEN

Montbrocq

Wittmann

A SQN

A COY

Tilly-sur-Seulles

Epinay

Amaye

M.Pelvey

VILLERS-BOCAGE
Wittmann's Second Attack

Wittmann's second battle-run into Villers-Bocage passed the smouldering remains of the RHQ Sharpshooter tanks. Dyas' wrecked Cromwell is just short of the bend in the road. The other vehicles and the MkIV tank on the left are part of the German force which took over the town after the battle.

The same scene in 1998. The motorcycle passes the spot where Dyas' tank was destroyed.

himself passed Cotton's ambush but was disabled by a well-placed shot from the Queens anti-tank gun. Cotton's troop completed the destruction. Sergeant Bramall's 17-pounder Firefly destroyed the second Tiger; Corporal Horne, having missed the Mk4 with his first shot, motored out into the main street and knocked-out the German tank with a shot in its vulnerable rear. The third Tiger was also destroyed, in one of the smaller streets just to the south.

Among the locals in Villers-Bocage that day was the son of the owner of the Château de Villers, just south of the town. Although the family had been allowed to stay in a wing of their home, the Château had been used as a German HQ throughout the war. On 13 Jun Count Stanislas de Clermont-Tonnerre, aware of the intense fighting, had donned his Red Cross arm-band and gone into the town to see whether he could help with any casualties. He watched Wittmann's second battle-run down the main street. When the German tank was hit and the crew started to clamber out, he ran forward to help the injured. As he helped the uninjured Wittmann to the ground he asked whether it was not rather rash to take on the British almost alone. 'Certainly not', replied Wittmann, 'I knew that the others would follow me', and he and his crew, like Dyas before him,

Wittmann's knocked out tiger in Villers-Bocage Main Street. Note the effects of the RAF bombing which obliterated the town after the battle.

After the fighting – the main street of Villers-Bocage. Wittmann's Tiger is in the foreground with a further knocked-out Tiger down the street alongside a wrecked MkIV.

Villers-Bocage main street, looking east, 1998. Both of Wittmann's battle-runs came down this street. The town has been completely rebuilt so it is impossible to pin-point the location of Wittmann's Tiger when it was destroyed.

disappeared into the back-streets of the town to make good their escape. De Clermont-Tonnerre was struck by the confidence, indeed haughty arrogance, of the German.

By now the rifle companies of 1/7 Queens were arriving. Gordon quickly deployed them – not a moment too soon. The Germans, too, were amassing forces. The Tiger tanks of Captain Mobius' 1 Company 101 SS Heavy Tank Battalion had arrived from Noyers-Boacge, about five miles north-east, and been joined by infantry from 2 Panzer Division and a few Mk4 tanks from Panzer Lehr which happened to be nearby. This force started to infiltrate the town from the east just as Gordon and his Queensmen established their defences near the western end. As the afternoon wore on tank-hunting and infiltration parties of both sides clashed in the streets of Villers-Bocage. It became a 'soldiers' battle, in which tenacity and fighting qualities counted most, and in which a colonel could be as personally involved as a private, as Colonel Gordon, on meeting a Tiger tank in one of the streets, recounts:

> 'This was altogether too much for me. I am ashamed to say that I grabbed a PIAT Team and rushed into a nearby shop to see if we could get a shot at the Tiger from a first floor window – not really, I suppose, what a battalion commander ought to do. I remember the appalled faces of the owners, particularily as we made a terrible mess of their bedroom when we fired. But PIATs were notoriously inaccurate and unreliable, and the round fell short. We moved quickly to another house which was nearer the Tiger, which now seemed to be stationary. We hit it with two shots, but seemed to do absolutely no damage at all – most frustrating. Perhaps we shook up the crew a bit, gave them a headache or something, for the tank started to reverse away back round the bend.'

But, while the Germans seemed prepared to throw in more troops in an attempt to seize the town, 1/7 Queens and the battered remains of the Sharpshooters were left to their own devices. Doubtless the absence of Brigadier Hinde, whose whereabouts throughout much of the day remains a mystery, explains the lack of decision and command by the British. As the afternoon wore on, Gordon, who had established his command post near the road junction where Wittmann had encountered Sergeant Lockwood, realised that the enemy were getting stronger, and that unless he was reinforced, his battalion must either pull back or eventually be over-run. This must be a decision for the brigade commander. Leaving his second-in-command, Major Griffiths, in temporary command, Gordon drove back in his jeep to see Hinde, who was now back at Brigade HQ west of the town. He explained the situation very clearly and stated that he and his Queensmen were quite prepared to fight to the last round, if that was what Hinde required. But if Hinde wanted to pull them out, he must give the order quickly, before the situation in Villers-Bocage became so confused, with hand-to-hand fighting in the streets against an ever-increasing enemy, that orderly withdrawal would be impossible. Hinde did not delay; 'Well, Desmond, its no good trying to win a VC here. Pull the battalion back while you still have tight control of them'.

After quickly locating a new position on the high-ground near Amayé, west of the town, Gordon returned to his command post in Villers-Bocage, sent Griffiths back to prepare the new position and gave orders for the withdrawal. It was shortly after 2000 on 13 June that Gordon stood at the road junction and watched his companies withdraw. 'First bloody time the Queens have ever had to retreat,' growled one soldier as he passed his commanding officer. 'And I very much hope it'll be the last,' replied Gordon. By 2020 the British had left Villers-Bocage – to which they did not return for nearly two months.

The night passed quietly for Gordon and his battalion, but at dawn the Germans attacked. Halted by well-controlled artillery fire, they were put to flight when Major Reid, one of the Queens company commanders, reacting quickly to the moment of indecision in the attack when the pendulum of battle seemed to hang limp, suddenly led his company in a fierce counter-attack. There were sporadic German attacks throughout 14 June, but none managed to penetrate the British position, and by nightfall the attacks seemed to have petered out completely. However, at a meeting that afternoon, General Bucknall, commander of XXX Corps, decided that progress by 50 Division in the Lingèvres area (see Chapter 8) had been insufficient to allow a link-up between it and 7 Armoured Division, whose position, some six miles further south, was now somewhat isolated and vulnerable to German attack. 22 Armoured Brigade must withdraw overnight 14/15 June. To many, including Gordon, this was an extremely disappointing decision. Convinced that they could have held on indefintely, if reinforced, Gordon considered that a strong position held in the area of Amayé would have posed a huge threat to the Germans, forcing Panzer Lehr Division to withdraw or be cut off, and providing a strongly-held launch-pad for future operations deep in enemy territory.

Often it is the commander who keeps his nerve and the soldier who goes on fighting longest who win the day. In his splendid anthology, *Other Men's Flowers*, Field Marshal Earl Wavell records his favourite military maxim, 'Man cannot tell, but Allah knows, how much the other side was hurt'. He suggests that 'when things are going badly in battle the best tonic is to take one's mind off one's own troubles by considering what a rotten time one's opponent must be having'. The Germans were certainly 'having a rotten time'. By the end of the battle the wreckage of six Tiger tanks

For his action at Villers-Bocage Michael Wittmann was awarded Cross Swords to the Knights Cross of the Iron Cross and promoted to *Hauptsturmführer* (captain). He was killed, along with his crew, 8 August 1944 south of Caen.

lay in the streets of Villers-Bocage – nearly half the fighting strength of 101 SS Heavy Tank Battalion. They had thrown everything available into the battle, and now had no further reserves upon which to call. Of course they had the advantage of the Tiger tank, but they won, not because their soldiers fought better, but because the nerve of their commanders lasted longer. They also had, in Michael Wittmann, a supremely brave soldier and a junior commander who always sought to impose his personality on the battlefield – at Villers-Bocage with devastating results.

It is very easy for the post-war, arm-chair tactician, with the advantage of hindsight, to criticise those who had responsibilities for taking decisions in battle – easy, usually unwise, and often unkind. The Sharpshooters leading squadron had certainly been destroyed. But the other squadrons and 1/7 Queens were still an effective fighting force. And 22 Armoured

Major-General Desmond Gordon (in the 1970s).

Brigade still had 5 RTR uncommitted. Behind them was 131 Brigade, with one armoured regiment and two lorried infantry battalions which General Erskine, commander of 7 Armoured Division, could have sent forward. And further back still, General Bucknall had 49 Infantry Division uncommitted. It seems a pity that the destruction of just one part of one regimental battlegroup was allowed to over-ride the fact that there were at least another ten battlegroups which could have joined the fray, perhaps decisively. The British senior commanders seem to have been so obsessed with their own problems that they had little time to consider the greater worries which con-fronted 'the other side'. One cannot help wondering how the battle of Normandy might have fared if more aggressive and confident leadership at brigade, division and corps level had been displayed on 13 June.

Perhaps an opportunity was lost. And perhaps it is not unrelated that by the time the British were finally to capture Villers-Bocage on 4 August, General Bucknall of XXX Corps, General Erskine of 7 Armoured Division, and Brigadier Hinde of 22 Armoured Brigade had been removed from their posts. Colonel Desmond Gordon was also removed from his post – to be promoted to Brigadier and take command of 151 Infantry Brigade a few days after the Battle of Villers-Bocage.

On the afternoon of 14 June, and in an effort to cover the withdrawal of 7 Armoured Division from the disaster of Villers-Bocage, the town was almost completely destroyed by Allied bombers. Hardly a building survived.

CHAPTER EIGHT

THE CAPTURE OF LINGÈVRES – 14 JUNE, D+8

Lingèvres lies 7 miles south of Bayeux, on the D13 just west of Tilly-sur-Seulles. Bayeux had been captured by 50 (Northumbrian) Division, almost unopposed, on 7 June. The division had then advanced south-east towards Tilly. On 8 June, Panzer Lehr Division, one of the strongest and best armoured divisions in the German Army, arrived in the area after a hurried move from Chartres. Tilly was to be the fulcrum for much heavy fighting in the following weeks. The Germans used it as a launch-pad for attacks against the British, while for the British it became an important objective on the route towards Villers-Bocage and beyond. On 10 and 11 June 7 Armoured Division advanced on Tilly before, halted by fierce resistance in the area of Bucéels, it was redirected on the right hook which was to end in the disaster of Villers-Bocage on 13 June.

There was fierce fighting in the area of Lingèvres and Verrières, one mile to the north-east, on 12 and 13 June as the British tried to break through the German positions and push on south to link up with 7 Armoured Division's advance on Villers-Bocage. But the defence of Panzer Lehr's 901 Panzer-Grenadier Regiment held. On 14 June 151 Infantry Brigade of 50 Division was ordered to take these two villages. 151 Brigade consisted of three battalions of The Durham Light Infantry – 6, 8, and 9 DLI; tough Geordies, many of them from northern mining families. 6 DLI, with B Squadron 4th/7th Dragoon Guards, was to capture Verrières on the left. On the right Lingèvres was the objective of 9 DLI with A Squadron of 4/7 DG.

One glance at Lingèvres today shows that it has been largely rebuilt. This is hardly surprising – the war caught up with Lingèvres with fearsome brutality on 14 June 1944. But the basic configuration of the village remains unchanged, centred round its sturdy stone church, with the war memorial beside it. This was to be the centre of the battle. At the west end of the church is a small turning to the right, signed to

Rotting carcasses of dead cows – a typical field in Normandy in the summer of 1944.

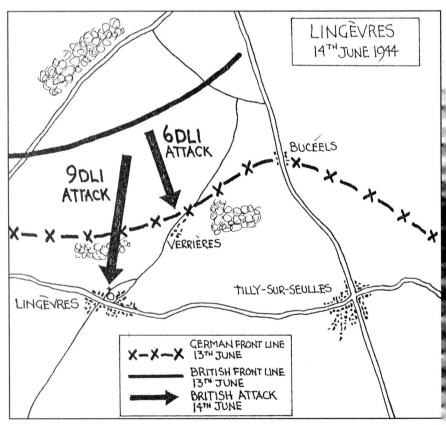

LINGÈVRES
14TH JUNE 1944

6DLI
ATTACK

9DLI
ATTACK

BUCÉELS

VERRIÈRES

LINGÈVRES

TILLY-SUR-SEULLES

X—X—X GERMAN FRONT LINE
13TH JUNE

BRITISH FRONT LINE
13TH JUNE

BRITISH ATTACK
14TH JUNE

Jouaye-Mondaye and Bayeux. **Follow this road** as it winds round a small field, over the stream, past a farm on the left and up a gentle rise, through typical Normandy woods and orchards, until you reach a small road and track junction in the middle of open fields, just half a mile from the village. Stop here and turn to face Lingèvres. You are now standing just forward of the British positions on the morning of 14 June 1944. The fields around you were 'no-man's land'.The Germans held the village and the woods north of it. But while everything is neat, tidy and prosperous today, the signs of war were obvious then. The road was unmetalled and churned up by the passage of many heavy military vehicles, so that the fields were covered with a thick layer of dust for several yards on either side. Smashed branches disfigured the trees, and the telephone lines hung down in loose tangles from broken poles. The most unpleasant and inescapable evidence of destruction was provided by the large number of dead cows which littered the fields. Killed by shellfire, blast or stray bullets, their carcasses lay rotting, till they swelled and finally burst, filling the summer air with that unique and sickly stench of death which lingers in the nostrils, and which no-

'A mighty concentration of fire.' The 5.5 inch guns of 84 Medium Regiment Royal Artillery provided fire support for the attack on Lingèvres.

one who fought in the Normandy campaign will ever forget. This was the scene for the battle for Lingèvres.

H Hour for the British attack was 1015. This was selected to ensure that 151 Brigade had the support of all the artillery that was in range – six field regiments, three medium regiments and one heavy regiment. On the right of 151 Brigade, 231 Brigade would also attack, at 1130, at which time this vast weight of artillery support would switch to support them.

9 DLI, commanded by Lieutenant Colonel Humphrey Wood, was an experienced and battle-hardened battalion, having fought in the Western Desert and Sicily. Since landing in Normandy a week earlier the battalion had been held in reserve. Indeed the only casualty sustained so far had been one sergeant drowned as they crossed the beach. This was to be their first taste of fighting in the 'bocage', its extensive cover and short fields of fire demanding quite different tactics from those required by the open spaces of the desert. The Geordies were about to learn the hard way.

Colonel Wood had sent out a few hastily-briefed patrols during the previous night, but, with so few hours of darkness in mid June, it had proved impossible to pinpoint the German positions, even though one patrol had managed to reach the edge of the village. Perhaps another 24 hours of patrolling and observation might have unlocked some of the secrets of the defences, but war seldom seems to offer the luxury of time. A decision by some senior commander that a place must be captured is almost always followed by a mad rush by those selected to carry out the attack. As with Hastings and the Green Howards' attack up the Sunken Lane onto Point 102 before, so Wood and the Durhams must launch their attack with insufficient time to find out what confronted them.

Time, however, is usually much kinder to the defender, and 901 Panzer-Grenadier Regiment had used it well. They had cleared the approaches to the woods and orchards around Lingèvres and sited automatic weapons to bring down a deadly cross-fire onto these killing areas. Perhaps, if the Durhams had known more of the defences or had already tasted the problems of fighting in the 'bocage', they might have suggested to their brigade commander that a different plan, perhaps even a night attack, was adopted. But Wood was given little scope for

British infantry advance – a Bren light machine gunner accompanied by two riflemen with bayonets fixed.

ingenuity. He produced a simple plan. The battalion would advance in box formation, using the road as the centre-line of the attack. A Company would lead on the left; C on the right. Behind them the two reserve companies, B and D respectively, would be prepared to pass through the leading companies on the order of the commanding officer. Wood himself would travel behind A Company on the left, while his second-in-command, Major John Mogg, would follow C Company on the right.

Unlike the Durhams, A Squadron 4/7DG, commanded by Major Jackie d'Avigdor-Goldsmid, had been in action almost continuously since landing on D Day. The learning curve rises very sharply in battle, if you are to survive for long. 4/7DG had learnt much about the reality of war in that one week. From time to time officers and NCOs had to get out of their tanks to contact the infantry they were supporting. Anything that identified a commander attracted the German snipers in the close bocage country. So, map boards were dispensed with; brass badges of rank had been replaced by less obvious cloth; field glasses were stuffed down into tank overalls. A half turret flap was always left open, but commanders did not stay for long with their

'Long lines of men advanced through the high corn, rifles pointing diagonally towards the sky.'

heads out of the turret. The regiment had developed excellent techniques for co-operating with the infantry. Infantrymen carried yellow fluorescent nylon triangles which, if need arose, could be strapped to a soldier's pack so that supporting aircraft could pick out the forward line of friendly troops. They proved to have an admirable second use. When pinned down, a yellow blob, tied to a rifle barrel and waved above the corn, was an excellent way for the infantryman to indicate to a nearby tank crew where the enemy fire was coming from. And the tank crews had developed an effective way of dealing with enemy infantry in ditches or trenches – a manner which appeared in no official Manual of Instruction! On the 75mm shell was a small switch which could be turned by a sixpence or screwdriver to activate a 'delay' mechanism. The gunner would then fire low, aiming to strike the hard ground some 20 yards short of the target. The round would ricochet about 10 feet into the air and explode in a deadly shrapnel burst above the heads of the enemy.

At 1015 9 DLI and A Squadron crossed their start-line, the forward edge of the woods about a mile north of Lingèvres, and began their advance across the open ground. Long lines of men advanced through the high corn, rifles pointing diagonally

Well-sited German machine-guns brought down a withering fire upon the advancing Durhams.

towards the sky. In front, columns of dust and masonry could be seen as the artillery subjected the village and neighbouring woods to a mighty concentration of fire, while overhead Typhoon aircraft added their rockets to the inferno. As always on such occasions it hardly seemed possible that any of the defenders could survive this terrible hammering.

But survive they did. As the leading companies neared the woods on the northern edge of the village the rolling artillery barrage moved forward. As it did so the Germans came to life. First two tanks opened fire, and were engaged by the Shermans of A Squadron. Then the well-sited German machine-guns, their arcs of fire linking across the open ground, brought down a withering fire upon the advancing Durhams. Men fell, including the two artillery Forward Observation Officers who were at the very front

'Typhoon aircraft added their rockets to the inferno' during the attack on Lingèvres.

of the attack, so that they could quickly switch artillery fire to neutralise troublesome enemy positions which threatened to hold up the advance.

On the left A Company, all their officers now casualties, ground almost to a halt. On the right C Company was still making progress, but slowly, with mounting casualties. Colonel Wood decided that the moment had come to push through his reserve companies. He told B Company to pass through A on the left, and take up the advance. No sooner had it done so than it, too, came under very heavy fire, losing all officers except one. It was clear that further advance on the left would be impossible. Wood therefore decided to switch the emphasis of the attack. He spoke to Major Mogg on the radio, ordered him to pass D Company through C on the right and to press on towards the village, while Wood himself tried to extricate A and B Companies and swing them round to the right as well. Barely had he given this order when a mortar bomb landed in the middle of his command group, killing Wood instantly and wounding his adjutant and signaller. Command of 9 DLI passed immediately to John Mogg.

Under Mogg's direction D and C Companies pressed on towards the village, supported by the tanks of A Squadron. One alert Sherman hull gunner noticed an anti-tank gun set back from the edge of the woods. He shot it up with long bursts from his Browning machine-gun, and the crew took to their heels, their long greatcoats flapping incongruously around their legs in the hot morning sunshine. Doggedly the Geordies fought their way forward towards the village against defenders who were just as determined not to give ground. There was much hand-to-hand fighting, but the Durhams would not be denied. As they overcame the German positions they realised how the enemy had survived the artillery bombardment – by attaching string to the triggers of their machine-guns so that they could still maintain a deadly fire while sheltering in the bottom of their trenches. Eventually, and much reduced in numbers, the Durhams managed to break into the village.

Drive back down the road into Lingèvres. Notice the delightful farmyard on your right, by the bend in the road, which now sells Normandy Cidre and Calvados. This became Mogg's HQ and the Regimental Aid Post of 9 DLI, once they had seized the village. It is hard to imagine, in that mile long journey through peaceful farmland, the grim reality of 9 DLI's advance on the morning of 14 June 1944. Shortly before your road joins the main road just short of the church, there is a small parking area on the right. Park there and walk the 50 yards to the church, on the wall of which is a plaque commemorating the actions of 50th (Northumbrian) Division in Normandy. Stand at the west end of the church, able to see the war memorial in front and the main D 13 running west out of the village. Try to re-create in your mind the scene of destruction that must have greeted the Durhams as, after a fearsome fight through the woods behind you, they eventually secured that Lingèvres cross-roads around midday on D+8.

A Squadron, whose supporting fire had been so important to the Durhams as they fought their way forward, was quick to follow the infantrymen into the village, their guns engaging any target that presented itself. Plumes of dust, rising from the unmetalled road as the tanks ground their way forward,

A Sherman moving up in support of the infantry passes a wrecked Mk IV.

mingled with the dust and smoke from the stricken village, making vision difficult for drivers, commanders and gunners. 2nd Troop, in the lead, was held up near the entrance to the village, so Major d'Avigdor-Goldsmid ordered 4th Troop to take the lead. As Lieutenant Alastair Morrison, commanding 4th Troop, halted alongside his squadron leader's tank, Goldsmid leant out and shouted, 'Get on up to the bend in the road, find the Infantry Sunray and take your orders from him'. (Sunray was a term used on the radio to denote a commander, without revealing his level of command). At the same time he told Captain John Stirling, A Squadron's second-in-command, to take the reserve troop and find a suitable position on the north-west edge of the village to guard against any enemy tank threat from the that direction.

Looking along the track Morrison could see the Durhams moving along the hedgerows towards the village. He ordered his driver to advance. As they approached the infantry a young captain stepped out from the side of the track and waved down the tank. Morrison stopped and jumped down from his tank. The captain was brief and to the point. 'We are going to capture the village and then hold it.' he said quickly, pointing towards the church, 'Give us maximum support. We are moving now.' Without waiting for a reply he hurried off to lead the attack. Nor was any discussion necessary. Morrison, now the 'veteran' of a week of continuous fighting, most of it in co-operation with infantry, knew exactly what was required. He climbed back into his Sherman and moved slowly down the road, followed by Corporal Johnson's tank, while Sergeant Harris, with his 17-pounder Firefly, covered them forward.

Morrison rounded the bend where the road drops down to the stream with the farm on the right. Ahead of them, through the smoke and dust of an almost completely destroyed village, he could see the infantrymen fighting their way forward. The weight of fire provided by tanks in close support of infantry is immense. The 75mm guns blasted holes in the houses, while the machine guns laid a blanket of fire on likely enemy positions. But it is not just the tanks' fire effect itself which is so valuable to assaulting infantry. Attacking a village like Lingèvres the infantryman feels especially vulnerable; every house can contain a sniper with his aim carefully laid. It is the threat to that sniper that the tank provides which most assures him. His confidence and morale are immeasurably increased by the presence of tanks in such a situation.

German mortar fire was coming down in the village, causing many casualties among the unprotected infantry. Shell splinters and bullets clanged off the tank's sides as Morrison manoeuvred his tank into a position near the church. He ordered Harris to cover the main road east towards Tilly while Johnson covered the road to Verrières, which, though under attack by 6 DLI, was still held by the enemy.

Breaking into the village may have been hard enough for the Durhams, but there was worse to come. They must now clear it and then hold it against enemy counter-attack. And 901 Panzer Grenadier Pegiment showed no intention of giving it up without a real fight. Every street, house and room had to be fought for. The battle for Lingèvres was to be long, bitter and confused, lasting all afternoon. The high, rapid zip of German Spandau fire contrasted with the slower hammering of the British Bren-guns and the frequent explosions of grenades. And clearly German artillery had the range of the village, as they

A Bren-gunner of the Durham Light Infantry.

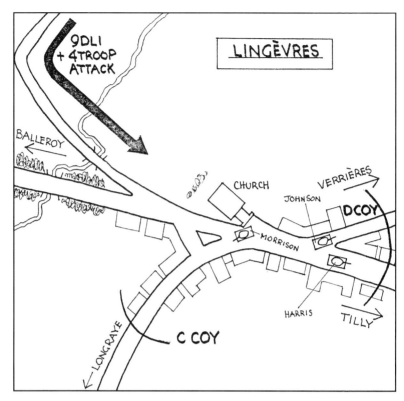

Lingèvres – the direction of the attack and positions taken up after the village had been taken.

fired high-explosive shells which burst in the air above the war memorial, showering shrapnel around and knocking slates and masonry off the church, were it fell on the luckless men below. Hot, dusty and exceedingly dangerous, the centre of Lingèvres was a most unhealthy place to be on the afternoon of 14 June 1944.

It was not long before action started at the east end of the village. From an excellent position behind the ruins of a cottage Sergeant Harris caught a glimpse of tank movement across a small valley. A minute later his 17-pounder gun fired and a Panther tank immediately burst into flames. This success was a real tonic for the infantry who were digging in in the area after their grim battle for the village. Shortly afterwards Goldsmid came on the radio to tell Morrison that 'Friendly Sunray is on his way up'. Morrison was to meet him at the western end of the chuch. Climbing out of his tank turret, Morrison jumped down and ran quickly into the church through a large hole that had been blown in the side wall. Nowhere was safe in Lingèvres, but at least by walking down the aisle to the west door he was afforded some protection by the solidly-built church walls.

Emerging through the west door, Morrison realised the real extent of the Durhams' casualties, which seemed to be ever increasing. Propped against the church wall, which was at least on the 'home' side of the village and therefore protected from small-arms fire, was a line of dead and wounded, which seemed constantly to increase as more casualties were brought in by men who then quickly returned to their area of responsibilty. As Morrison waited the arrival of 'the friendly Sunray' he saw a Bren-gun carrier race up the road by which 4th Troop had entered the village. The driver skid-turned his carrier on arrival and backed it in beside the church. Single-handed he loaded it with wounded men and then drove off – slowly, this time, so as not to jolt his passengers unnecessarily – back down the road to the large farmyard beside the bend in the road, where the Durham's Medical Officer had clearly established a make-shift Aid Post. The driver was to make this solitary and dangerous journey many times that afternoon, seemingly oblivious of the constant shelling. As afternoon drew towards evening the inevitable end came. The carrier stood stationary in the road, its devoted driver and his last cargo still and silent where a shell-

German 88mm gun firing in support of infantry.

The Regimental Aid Post of the Durhams, after the battle. The soldiers receiving treatment is a captured German.

burst had killed them all. Morrison never knew his name, but he never forgot that driver, nor the medical orderly who worked tirelessly throughout the day looking after casualties beside the church. These were among the unsung heroes of war – men who, regardless of their own safety, saved the lives of many, though eventually they lost theirs.

As Morrison stood by the church wall a tall, dust-covered, broad-shouldered major strode up the road towards him. There was an obvious air of authority about him – clearly this was the expected Sunray. 'Are you commanding the company here?' asked Morrison when they met. 'No,' said John Mogg with a grin, 'I'm bloody well commanding the battalion! Now, show me where your tanks are deployed.' His cheerful, unconcerned manner was a real tonic. After a short discussion Mogg walked on into the village, leaving the troop leader reassured that at least there was someone in Lingèvres who was about to take a firm grip on the battle.

Although Morrison did not know it, Mogg's air of easy confidence was based on sound training rather than previous combat experience. Unlike most of 9 DLI Mogg had not fought in the desert and Sicily. Indeed he had only joined the battalion as second-in-command one week before D Day from commanding a Battle School in England. This move had involved a change of cap badge as his original regiment was The Oxfordshire and Buckinghamshire Light Infantry. But he was not the sort of man to let lack of battle experience bother him, and he quickly imposed his personality on the battle of Lingèvres. By now most of the German infantry had been driven out of the village, so Mogg sent D Company to take up a position astride the road running east towards Tilly. Weakened by casualties, the company was now organised as two platoons, which were sited on either side of the road. C Company, now reduced to little over one platoon strength, was sent to do likewise on the Longraye road to the south, while A and B Companies, which had suffered most heavily in the early advance across the open cornfields, were held in reserve near the back of the village.

Having assured himself that the defence was properly co-ordinated, Mogg went to find the artillery commander, Major Ken Swann. Together they worked out a defensive fire plan for the village. This was to prove invaluable throughout the rest of the day as Swann ensured that every German counter-attack was greeted with quick, heavy and accurate artillery fire. (Major Swann was killed three days later. His grave, with many of the others who died in Lingèvres that day, is in the Commonwealth War Graves Commission Cemetery at Tilly-sur-Seulles.) Mogg's final task was to call up the battalion's anti-tank guns and place them to cover all the roads leading into the village.

From his position near the church Morrison watched the anti-tank guns arrive; 6-pounder guns towed by high-sided carriers called Dragons. Two of these rumbled laboriously by, on their way to join C Company on the Longraye road. On arrival the crews unhitched the guns and sited them facing down the road, before stacking boxes of ammunition in the nearby doorways. Hardly had they done so, and the Dragons withdrawn, when there was a loud 'crump' from the direction of Tilly. Morrison looked up to see one of the guns lying on its side in the ditch, its crew dead beside it. A second 'crump', and the second gun and its crew were flung into the air like discarded toys. Almost immediately Sergeant Harris, who was covering east, reported on the radio that he thought he could see a tank approaching from Tilly. A few seconds later he confirmed excitedly that it was indeed a tank, moving very fast, and that it seemed to be a Sherman. Soon Morrison could see it too; definitely a Sherman, presumably from B Squadron, which was supporting 6 DLI's attack on Verrières, and had over-run its objective. Suddenly, and shortly before reaching the village, the Sherman swung sharp right up a track, revealing, close behind it, a German Panther. Harris was not fooled. He gave a quick order to Trooper MacKillop his gunner and a round from the 17-pounder smashed into the Panther, knocking off a track and sending it swerving into the hedge beside the road, where it lay canted at an angle half off the road.

MacKillop's shot had disabled the Panther, but not put its gun out of action. Mogg considered that it still posed a real threat which must be dealt with. It would clearly be unwise for Harris' tank to drive openly down the road to engage it; it was a job for the Durhams. He decided to take out a tank-hunting party himself, with a sergeant and private from the nearby D Company and a PIAT anti-tank weapon. Stealthily and slowly they crept towards the disabled tank until they got within about 15 yards of it, undetected. Instructed by Mogg the PIAT-gunner balanced his weapon on a convenient bank. 'Right,' said Mogg tensely, ' When I say 'fire', fire!' The Geordie looked at him with horror, and eventually mumbled: 'But I don't know how to fire the bloody thing, sir!'

Mogg could hardly believe his ears – perhaps the man had collected the PIAT from another who had become a casualty earlier. He looked at the sergeant; 'I can't either, sir!' Mogg made a few terse comments as he shouldered the PIAT himself, took careful aim and, with fingers mentally crossed, squeezed the trigger. There was an instantaneous and satisfactory 'woomph' as the tank blew up in a sheet of flame. Two German troopers clambered hastily out, dropped to the ground and started to run away. Mogg drew his pistol and fired a few parting shots, which missed, he later admitted, but probably hastened them on their way. He then followed his two companions who were already sprinting back along the road towards the main position. It was hardly, thought Mogg as he recovered his breath, the sort of activity in which a battalion commander ought to be involved, but was perhaps justified in view of the end result and the boost that it gave to D Company's morale.

Others were tank-hunting, too, if rather less successfully. Lieutenant Ken Whittaker, the Durham's anti-tank platoon commander, had noticed, while siting one of his guns, a Panther tank in a barn down the Longraye road. Tank-hunting is not a role for a towed anti-tank gun, which must be dragged into position by its Dragon tractor, unhitched and turned round before it can engage a target. Whittaker returned quickly to the middle of the village and sought out a convenient tank to engage the Panther. Here he met Major d'Avigdor-Goldsmid, who had just arrived near the church. Goldsmid decided that he

British soldiers operating a PIAT in Normandy. 'But I don't know how to fire the bloody thing, sir!'

must establish exactly what and where his target was before he set out to stalk it. The two officers undertook a joint reconnaissance on foot. They crept past the two 6-pounder anti-tank guns which had been destroyed earlier, with the crews still lying dead beside them, and approached the barn. Sure enough, the Panther was still there, and, to the utter astonishment of Goldsmid and Whittaker, beside it stood a German soldier calmly shaving. They withdrew quietly and hatched a plan. Whittaker and a patrol of infantry would work their way round the left flank while Goldsmid's tank moved along the narrow track that ran behind the barn. On a given signal the infantry would fire a PIAT at short range, while the tank would fire at a point on the barn wall on the other side of which Goldsmid judged the Panther would be. The signal was duly given. The PIAT, a notoriously unreliable weapon, misfired, while the Sherman fired three rounds in quick succession. To their joint dismay the Panther rolled out of the barn and made off towards the open country, apparently unscathed.

A Squadron suffered its first casualty of the day shortly afterwards. A Durham corporal told Morrison that he could hear the sounds of tracked vehicles to the south. Corporal Johnson, whose tank was now covering that direction, could see nothing, so Morrison ordered him to move to where he could get a better view down the Longraye road. No sooner had Johnson moved forward than his tank was struck by an armoured-piercing round. Luckily the Sherman did not catch fire, but the shot had disabled it. Johnson climbed out badly wounded. He died of his wounds the following day. As the radio operator, Lance Corporal Draper, scrambled down the back of the tank and hurried to take cover, he realised that the gun was off-centre, thereby preventing the driver, Trooper Dagley, from opening his hatch. Dagley, a quiet family man from the west country, had had a premonition that he would not return from Normandy. Before the invasion, when most soldiers were encouraged to send home all their unnecessary possessions, Dagley had also sent his most private and personal effects; watch, wallet and fountain-pen. In reply to Morrison's questions Dagley had explained that he came from a poor family and that as he would not be returning from the war it was important for his wife to have everything of value before he went. Morrison's assurances of likely survival made no

Lingèvres 1998. Looking east towards Tilly-sur-Sellies.

Corporal Johnson's Sherman beside Lingèvres Church, after the battle. Note the gun traversed so that it does not obstruct the driver's hatch.

impression. Now Dagley was trapped, possibly injured or even dead, in a disabled tank, in imminent danger of being hit again. Draper quickly realised the situation and, in full view of the enemy, ran back, climbed into the tank turret and traversed the gun until the driver's hatch was free. He then climbed out of the turret and opened the driver's hatch. But Dagley did not move. Draper pulled the driver out through the hatch and carried him, with some difficulty for Dagley was a big man, into the shelter of the church wall, bedside the other casualties. But it was in vain. Dagley's premonition had been correct; he died a few minutes later. (Trooper Dagley's grave is in the small cemetary of Jerusalem, an oasis of peace beside the busy Bayeux / Tilly - sur-Seulles road.) It is worth recording that Draper was not shot at as he carried out his rescue attempt. Morrison has always been convinced that this was because the enemy at Lingèvres was Panzer Lehr, a regular Wehrmacht division, not one of the SS formations.

This left Morrison short of one tank if he was to cover all the roads into Lingèvres. But he was surprised to find that another Sherman tank, apparently spare, had arrived in the centre of the village. This seemed to answer his problem. Clearly it did not belong to 4/7DG, but its ownership was irrelevant to Morrison, who wanted all the tank fire-power available to him. He climbed onto it and banged on the cupola, which opened to reveal the artillery battery commander, Major Swann. In reply to Morrison's request that he should cover the area south, Swann explained that to make room inside the turret for the many radio sets needed to control the artillery fire the gun had been removed and replaced by a wooden mock-up. A gunless tank, obviously bristling with radios, would be an immediate target for German gunners.

Further discussion seemed pointless, especially as the Germans chose that moment to launch a counter-attack against the village. This was beaten off by the Durhams and A Squadron, as were several other German attempts to recapture the village. Mogg and Morrison had good cause to be grateful for the presence of Major Swann, since the splendid artillery fire support played a vital part in dealing with each successive German attack.

By about 1630 tank gun ammunition was running low. That Sherman tanks carried 90 rounds gives an indication of the level of fighting in Lingèvres that day. Replenishment trucks were called forward and Goldsmid gave orders that tanks were to be withdrawn one by one to re-arm, re-fuel and then return to the village. First to go was Sergeant Harris; Morrison wanted his 17-pounder fully re-armed back in position as soon as possible. This proved to be a wise decision; no sooner had Harris returned and taken up a position near the village centre than events began to move very rapidly.

Goldsmid became increasingly concerned at reports from the infantry that there were tank noises on the road running west out of Lingèvres towards Balleroy. Tank commanders, with the noise of their tank engines and the continuous 'mush' of their radios, rely upon the ears of the infantry in situations like this. He told Captain John Stirling, who was in position providing flank protection about a quarter of a mile north-west of the village, to investigate. Stirling went alone, unsupported, and before long he reported that he could see the outline of a Panther turret on the road out of Lingèvres. He proposed to deal with it. This required considerable care; Stirling's tank only had a 75mm gun against which a Panther was almost invulnerable unless hit in the right place. Conversely, one shot from the Panther would certainly destroy the Sherman. Using the available cover, Stirling skillfully stalked his prey until, at about 400 yards range, he considered that he was in position. He carefully laid the gun himself, aiming at a hedge just below the Panther's turret. Three quick rounds of solid shot from the Sherman into the Panther's vulnerable side and the unsuspecting German tank immediately started to brew. '16, I've got it, and its starting to brew.' Stirling's voice was exultant

German infantry moving up for an attack.

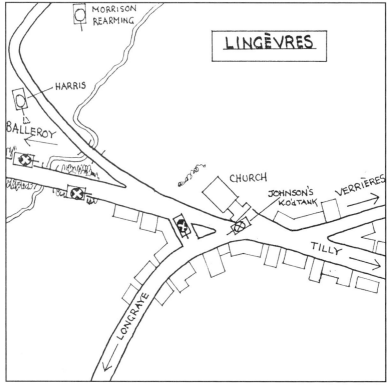

Lingèvres – showing the three Panthers knocked-out by Harris.

over the squadron radio.

Meanwhile Goldsmid had prudently summoned Harris and re-sited his tank so that it covered the road past the church. He was only just in time. The effect of Stirling's strike was electrifying. This tank proved to be the last of a group of four. Seeing the back tank so suddenly and unexpectedly destroyed the remaining three immediately bolted east towards the village in a bid to escape. In the village the cry of 'Tank coming; Tank coming' went up. As ever, Harris was ready. As the leading Panther swept down the road his gunner, Trooper MacKillop knocked it out with a single shot. Fifty yards behind a second Panther roared past the crouching Durhams. It met the same fate and quickly burst into flames. The 17-pounder gun was really proving its worth. Two crew members jumped out, their clothes alight; no-one shot at them. Unbelievably a third Panther was hot on its tail and thundered into the village flat

The last of the Panther tanks knocked out by Sergeant Harris beside the war memorial in Lingèvres.

Lingèvres 1998. The war memorial still bears the marks of the battle. The small turning to the right, off the main road, was the axis up which 9 DLI and 4/7 DG entered the village.

The morning after! A soldier of the 9 DLI examines on of the Panther tanks knocked out by Sergeant Harris at the western end of Lingèvres. Another wrecked Panther can be seen on the other side of the road.

Inset: Lingèvres in 1998.

out. It managed to avoid its two predecessors, which had skidded into the ditches on opposite sides of the road, and, as it reached the middle of the village, McKillop just had time to fire another shot. This blasted the sprocket off its near side, and it slewed to a halt beside the war memorial. A total of six Panther tanks now lay smouldering in Lingèvres, five of them victims of the coolness and accuracy of Harris and McKillop, both of whom were later decorated; Harris was awarded The Distinguished Conduct Medal, while McKillop was Mentioned in Despatches.

(Perhaps surprisingly the exact locations of two of Sergeant Harris' victims can still be seen. Walk down the D13, westwards from the church. After a few hundred yards there is a small culvert, seen clearly in the photographs of 1944 and today. Just short of it on the left, and beyond it on the right, are gaps in the hedges which exactly correspond with the locations of the Panther tanks.)

This dramatic episode marked the finale of the battle for Lingèvres. From this moment the firing seemed to die away. The Durham infantrymen emerged from the rubble; the tank crews climbed out of their tanks. Someone found a crate of champagne on the back of one of the destroyed Panthers and the tension relaxed. The village was held, but the cost had been high. 9 DLI lost 22 officers and 226 men in Lingèvres on 14 June 1944. Among the decorations won that day was a DSO for Major John Mogg – later in the campaign he was to win a bar to that award, and MCs to Major Jackie d'Avigdor-Goldsmid and Lieutenant Alastair Morrison of A Squadron 4/7DG.

A few days later a new brigadier took over command of 151 Brigade – Brigadier Desmond Gordon, hot-foot from commanding 1/7 Queens at Villers-Bocage (see Chapter 7). He did not wait long before confirming Major John Mogg as the commanding officer of 9DLI, in the rank of Lieutenant-Colonel.

General Montgomery invests Lieutenant-Colonel John Mogg with the DSO. Awarded after the battle for Lingèvres.

APPENDICES

Appendix A: ORDER OF BATTLE—ALLIED FORCES

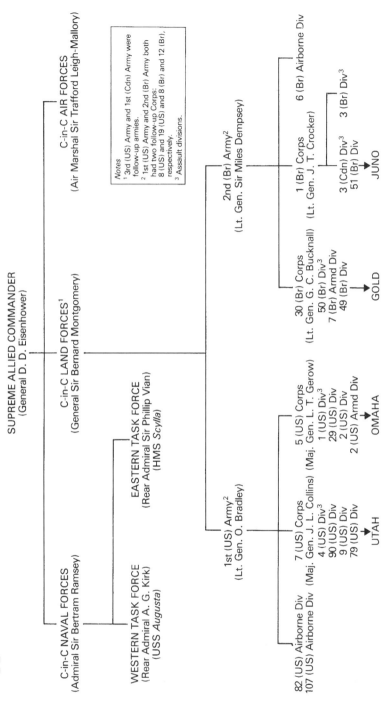

SUPREME ALLIED COMMANDER
(General D. D. Eisenhower)

C-in-C NAVAL FORCES
(Admiral Sir Bertram Ramsey)

C-in-C LAND FORCES[1]
(General Sir Bernard Montgomery)

C-in-C AIR FORCES
(Air Marshal Sir Trafford Leigh-Mallory)

Notes
[1] 3rd (US) Army and 1st (Cdn) Army were follow-up armies.
[2] 1st (US) Army and 2nd (Br) Army both had two follow-up Corps: 8 (US) and 19 (US) and 8 (Br) and 12 (Br), respectively.
[3] Assault divisions.

WESTERN TASK FORCE
(Rear Admiral A. G. Kirk)
(USS *Augusta*)

EASTERN TASK FORCE
(Rear Admiral Sir Phillip Vian)
(HMS *Scylla*)

1st (US) Army[2]
(Lt. Gen. O. Bradley)

2nd (Br) Army[2]
(Lt. Gen. Sir Miles Dempsey)

7 (US) Corps
(Maj. Gen. J. L. Collins)
4 (US) Div[3]
90 (US) Div
9 (US) Div
79 (US) Div
→ UTAH

5 (US) Corps
(Maj. Gen. L. T. Gerow)
1 (US) Div[3]
29 (US) Div
2 (US) Div
2 (US) Armd Div
→ OMAHA

30 (Br) Corps
(Lt. Gen. G. C. Bucknall)
50 (Br) Div[3]
7 (Br) Armd Div
49 (Br) Div
→ GOLD

1 (Br) Corps
(Lt. Gen. J. T. Crocker)
3 (Cdn) Div[3]
51 (Br) Div
→ JUNO

82 (US) Airborne Div
107 (US) Airborne Div

6 (Br) Airborne Div
3 (Br) Div[3]
3 (Br) Div

SECTOR	AMERICAN		BRITISH		
BEACH	UTAH	OMAHA	GOLD	JUNO	SWORD
	'U'	'O'	'G'	'J'	'S'
NAVAL ASSAULT FORCE					
NAVAL COMMANDER	Rear Admiral D. P. Moon (USS Bayfield)	Rear Admiral J. L. Hall (USS Ancon)	Commodore C. E. Douglas-Pennant (HMS Bulolo)	Commodore G. N. Oliver (HMS Hilary)	Rear Admiral A. G. Talbot (HMS Largs)
ASSAULT DIVISION	4 (US) Div (7 Corps)	1 (US) Div (5 Corps)	50 (BR) Div (30 Corps)	3 (CDN) Div (1 Corps)	3 (BR) Div (1 Corps)
DIVISIONAL COMMANDER	Major General R. O. Barton	Major General C. R. Heubner	Major General D. A. H. Graham	Major General R. F. L. Keller	Major General T. G. Rennie
MISSION	To establish a bridgehead along the line Quinéville-Ste Mere Eglise—north of Carentan and link up with 101 (US) Airborne Div	To establish control of RN 13 between Isigny and Bayeux. Two battalions allotted for the capture of Pointe du Hoc	To capture Bayeux and establish a position across RN 13 and ensure liaison with flanking divisions	To establish a bridgehead 18 km deep seizing the heights west of Caen around Carpiquet air field. 48 Cdo RM to protect the east flank by capturing Langrune-sur-Mer	To capture Caen as soon as possible and link up with 6 (Br) Airborne Div
LANDING AREA	From Dunes-de-Varreville to 2 km to the south	Between Pointe et Raz de la Percée and Sainte-Honorine	Between Le Hamel and la Rivière	Between Vaux and Saint-Aubin	Between Lion-sur-Mer and Riva-Bella
TIME OF ASSAULT (H-HR)	0630	0630	0725	0745 (7 Bde) 0755 (8 Bde)	0730

Appendix C D-Day on the Beaches

UTAH

H-hour was several minutes late on Utah Beach. Two naval control vessels went missing and dust and smoke from the bombardment obscured the beach. As the landing-craft neared the shore strong coastal currents pushed them southwards, and the landing was eventually made two and a half kilometres south of the originally intended spot. As it turned out the defences at La Madeleine (la Grande Dune) were luckily far less than those on the original objectives.

From then on things went well for 4 (US) Division. By midday all resistance had been overcome for only light casualties, the beach was clear and the troops were moving inland. Resistance stiffened in the afternoon but by nightfall 23,250 men, 1,700 vehicles and 1,695 tons of stores had been landed over the beaches. Contact had been made with 82 Airbourne Division at Chef-du-Pont and a bridgehead established taking in Sainte-Mère-Église and a large pocket of land north of Carentan.

OMAHA

The sea was rough off Omaha and this made the landing extremely hazardous. Ten landing craft were sunk during the run-in to the beach and amny artillery pieces lost. Only 5 out of 32 amphibious tanks reached the beach after being launched five kilometeres from the shore. In the confusion many parties were landed on the wrong stretch of beach.

As the landing craft, water lapping over the gunwales, landed their troops, they were met by a hail of fire from strong enemy positions reinforced by troops of the 352 Division who were stationed nearby. Such was the strength of the defence that the 1 (US) Division could not force their way inland from the shoreline. Troops huddled for shelter under the high dunes as artillery fire pounded the beaches and machine guns whipped the sea into a foam. Successive waves, landing at their appointed time, added to the chaos on the beach, which soon became cluttered with burning vehicles and abandoned equipment. By 0930 hours the German commander at Points et Raz de la Percée judged that the landing would fail. Gradually, however, the tables turned. Small groups of gallant soldiers, supported by the fire of destroyers venturing dangerously close inshore, fought their way through the dunes and in the end sheer numbers and dogged perseverance told against the defenders. Futher along the coast at the Pointe du Hoc, 225 Ranger Battalion scaled the cliffs to destroy the battery, found it empty, discovered the cannon nearby, destroyed them and then came under severe counter-attack themselves. Less than 100 men in number, they held out for two days and nights before being relieved by troops from Omaha.

By the end of the day more than 34,000 Americans were crammed into a bridgehead only one or two kilometres deep and seven kilometres wide. They had suffered over 2,000 killed or wounded to achieve that much and their situation was precarious. Only one road inland was open. Only 100 tons of stores were ashore out of the 2,400 tons which the plan had called for. Ammunition was short, almost all the artillery and most of the tanks and vehicles had been sunk or knocked out. The Americans were ashore at Omaha - but only just. It was the beach on which the invasion came closest to failing.

GOLD

German resistance was strong and determined on Gold Beach as well as on Omaha. In the west it took 231 Brigade until late i the afternoon before they could capture the strongpoint at Le Hamel and, to the east, the capture of La Rivière cost 69 Brigade 94 men killed, including six officers. Aided by numerous extroadinery tanks carrying flails to explode mines, flame-throwers and obstacle breathing equipment, 50 Division established themselves ashore by the middle of the day and by nightfall had secured a firmbridgehead well inland. Nearly 25,00 men had been landed for the loss of 413 killed, missing or wounded and a link-up had been made with 3 (Canadian) Division to the east.

Betweeen Gold and Omaha, at the junction of the British and American sectors, 47 Commando, Royal Marines, were given the task of capturing Port-en-Bessin. After losing 43 men and all their signalling equipment when four of their landing crafft were sunk by underwater explosive devices, 47 Commando were unable to commence their attack on the port until the following morning. It fell on 8 June after the Commando had suffered 200 casualties.

JUNO

Progress on Juno beach was, as elsewhere, hampered by a high sea, submerged obstacles and a stiff resistance. Despite this, 3 (Canadian) Division had placed 21,400 men, 3,200 vehicles and 2,100 tons of stores on the shore by the end of the day. In the course of establishing their bridgehead the Canadians lost 304 killed, 574 wounded and 47 captured. Several strongpoints remained intact as D-Day ended and 48 Commando Royal Marines had failed to capture the strongpoint at Saint-Aubin. Nevertheless liason had been established with 50 Division to the east and the Canadians were firmly launched into France.

SWORD

3 (British) Division had a patchy but overall successful day. The mission of capturing Caen was not accomplished, but a substantial lodgement was achieved during the day despite a prolonged resistance from numerous strongpoints and a counter-attack during the evening from 21st Panzer Division. This division attacked with more than 100 tanks supported by two battalions of infantry in the 9 Brigade sector around Biéville and Périers. When the attack finally ran out of steam, around seven o'clock in the evening, more than 50 German tanks were left on the battlefield. Six Commando units were landed to capture isolated strongpoints between the main divisional beach and the area of the airbourne landings and were largely successful in achieving their missions.

By midnight on D-Day 28,845 men were ashore: 630 had been killed or wounded on the beaches alone.

Appendix D War Cemeteries in the Invasion Area

This is a list of the war cemeteries in the invasion area (the number of graves are shown in brackets).

AMERICAN
    Saint Laurent   Overlooking Omaha Beach (9,814).

CANADIAN
    Bény-sur-Mer   On the D35 between Tailleville and Reviers, 10 miles north-west of Caen (2,049).

BRITISH AND ALLIES

Banneville-La-Campagne	Half a mile west of the village on the RN815, six miles east of Caen (4,648).
Bayeux	On the bypass south-west of the town (3,934 and 181 Canadian).
Brouay	In the churchyard of the village which is a mile south of the RN13, about midway between Byeux and Caen (377).
Cambes-en-Plaine	At the north of the village which is four miles north of Caen on the D7 (224).
Fontenay-Le-Pesnel	Fontenay is 10 miles west of caen on the D9 and the cemetery is three-quarters of a mile south of the village (519).
Hermanville	The village lies on the D35 a mile and a half to the west of Ouistreham and just inland fron the coast. The cemetery lies to the east of the church (1005).
Hottot-les-Bagues	Hottot-les-Bagues is nine miles south of Bayeux and the cemetery is a mile north-east of the village on the road to Caen (1137).
Jéruzalem, Chouain	Five miles south east of Bayeux on the road from there to Tilly-sur-Seulles (48).
La Délivrande, Douvres	Seven miles north of Caen on the road to Langrune (1123).
Ranville	By the church at Ranville. Seven miles north-east of Caen (2563).
Ryes, Bazenville	Two miles east of Ryes and five north-east of Bayeux (979).
Secqueville-en-Bessin	In the cemetery to the east of the village which is two miles north of the main-road and midway between Caen and Bayeux (117).
St Manvieu	Seven miles west of caen on the road from there to Caumont (2183).
Tilly-sur-Seulles	Half a mile west of Juvigny which lies seven miles south east of Bayeux (1222).

GERMAN
    La Cambe   On the RN13 between Bayeux and Isigny (20,507).

(Note: Additionally some Commonwealth cmeteries contain German graves, notably Bayeux, Ryes, La Délivrande and Ranville.)

The Cemetery at Jerusalem. Smallest of the Commonwealth War Graves cemeteries in Normandy with just 47 graves. It is a haven of peace and tranquillity beside the bustling D6 Bayeux to Tilly-sur-Seulles road. At the left end of the back row is the grave of Trooper Dagley, 4th Troop, A Squadron, 4th/7th Royal Dragoon Guards. He lies just three miles from the village of Lingèvres, where he died on 14 June 1944.

INDEX

FORMATIONS & UNITS

Allied

American

British & Canadian

German